Conquest

By
Mark Crawford

Copyright 2025 Mark Crawford. All rights reserved.

No part of this book may be reproduced in any form or by any electronic or mechanical means including information storage and retrieval systems, without permission in writing from the author. The only exception is by a reviewer, who may quote short excerpts in a review.

Although the author and publisher have made every effort to ensure that the information in this book was correct at press time, the author and publisher do not assume and hereby disclaim any liability to any party for any loss, damage, or disruption caused by errors or omissions, whether such errors or omissions result from negligence, accident, or any other cause.

This publication is designed to provide accurate and authoritative information with regard to the subject matter covered. It is sold with the understanding that the publisher is not engaged in rendering professional services. If legal advice or other expert assistance is required, the services of a competent professional should be sought.

The fact that an organization or website is referred to in this work as a citation and/or a potential source of further information does not mean that the author or the publisher endorses the information the organization or website may provide or recommendations it may make.

Please remember that Internet websites listed in this work may have changed or disappeared between when this work was written and when it is read.

Conquest

Table of Contents

Introduction 1
Chapter 1: Understanding Our Identity in Christ 4
    Embracing the Role of a Conqueror 5
    Biblical Foundations of Conquest 7
Chapter 2: Overcoming a Passive Mindset 10
    Recognizing Spiritual Complacency... 11
    Strategies for Living Proactively 14
Chapter 3: Advancing the Kingdom of God 17
    Taking Initiative in Faith 17
    Engaging in Spiritual Warfare 20
Chapter 4: Empowered by the Holy Spirit 24
    Gifts and Fruits of the Spirit.. 25
    Listening to and Following Divine Guidance 28
Chapter 5: Building a Strong Prayer Life 32
    The Importance of Consistent Prayer 32
    Effective Prayer Strategies.. 35
Chapter 6: The Role of Community and Fellowship 39
    Strength in Unity 39
    Building Supportive Christian Relationships 42
Chapter 7: Navigating Challenges and Trials 47
    Finding Strength in Adversity 47
    Maintaining Faith Through Difficulties...................................... 49

Chapter 8: The Power of Testimony 52
    Sharing Personal Faith Experiences 52
    Encouraging Others Through Storytelling 55

Chapter 9: Living Faith in Action 58
    Demonstrating Faith Through Works 58
    Impacting Society as a Believer 61

Chapter 10: Managing Spiritual and Emotional Health 64
    Balancing Faith Life with Self-Care 64
    Recognizing and Overcoming Spiritual Burnout 67

Chapter 11: Embracing Lifelong Growth 70
    Continuous Learning and Development 70
    Staying Relevant in a Changing World 74

Chapter 12: Preparing for Eternal Victory 77
    Understanding the Promise of Eternal Life 77
    Living with an Eternal Perspective 80

Conclusion 84

Introduction

If you've ever found yourself imagining the life of a Christian as a peaceful meander through life's peaks and valleys, relying solely on faith while humming "Que Sera, Sera," you're not alone. This picturesque notion can be comforting, but it may also lull us into a passive mindset. The truth is, while our walk with Christ offers peace and assurance, it also calls us to arms—not with swords and shields, but with spiritual grit and determination.

Consider the notion of life as a passive observer, drifting downstream like a leaf carried by the currents. This image seems serene, yet it's not the life we're called to. Instead, we are summoned to become proactive and diligent stewards of our faith. Being a Christian is not about hiding behind the walls of complacency or being caught in the web of inactivity. It's about living with a vibrant sense of purpose, fueled by the promises of God.

Christians, young and old, new or seasoned in the faith, share a mandate that transcends the boundaries of age and circumstance. We are all called to be more than just believers—we are called to be conquerors. As it is written, "Yet, in all these things we are more than conquerors through him that loved us" (Rom. 8:37). While the journey may not always be smooth, it promises the kind of fulfillment that wooden pews can't quite encapsulate.

To embrace the role of a conqueror is an invitation to challenge the status quo within ourselves. It asks us to confront notions of complacency and reassess our approach to faith. This book aims to awaken within us a renewed understanding of what it means to be active participants in our spiritual journey. Through humor, wisdom, and biblical truths, we'll explore a life marked by purposeful action and unshakeable faith.

But let's not confuse this with an impractical, pie-in-the-sky optimism. The Christian journey is punctuated with trials and tribulations, sometimes feeling like we're mere spectators in the theater of life. And yet, amidst these challenges, lies the heart of being conquerors—not in avoiding difficulties but in facing and overcoming them through His strength. The scripture reminds us, "I can do all things through Christ who strengthens me" (Phil. 4:13), serving as a powerful testament to the resilience that faith provides.

This introduction isn't just the beginning of a book—it's the beginning of a mindset shift. It's a call to roll up our spiritual sleeves and take part in a grand adventure, fueled by faith and boundless divine potential. Our identities in Christ equip us for this very task. Here, we lay the groundwork for understanding and executing our roles within God's Kingdom.

Throughout the pages that follow, you will find encouragement and practical wisdom aimed at extinguishing passivity and igniting a proactive faith. With divine inspiration, we'll learn to embrace our God-given identities, advancing His Kingdom with purpose and passion. From understanding the power of prayer to navigating life's inevitable challenges, each chapter is designed to build upon the last, creating a cohesive blueprint for Christian living.

The tone here is not one of reprimand but of motivation, infused with light-hearted humor that makes the serious endeavor of spiritual growth accessible and engaging. We draw inspiration from the dynamic and often colorful characters within the pages of the Bible, who remind us that faith is an active force. The stories within the holy text are not static tales of past glories but living instructions for victory in our current battles.

Conquest

And so, as we embark on this journey together, we arm ourselves with more than just biblical knowledge; we embrace a lifestyle that exudes faith in action. This isn't a path traveled solo—it's one that thrives on community and fellowship. Together, we find strength, share testimonies, and uplift one another, echoing the call in Ecclesiastes: "Two are better than one; because they have a good reward for their labour" (Eccl. 4:9).

Ultimately, this introduction serves as a rallying cry. It is your invitation to strip away any remnants of a passive life and step boldly into the future as active conquerors of faith. So, before we dive into the chapters ahead, let's center our hearts and minds, remembering that this journey is divinely powered by a God who equips us for whatever lies ahead. "For with God, nothing shall be impossible" (Luke 1:37). Let's accept the challenge and live life not as passive recipients but as empowered conquerors in Christ.

Chapter 1:
Understanding Our Identity in Christ

Let's dive right in and shake off any lingering doubts. Understanding our identity in Christ is pivotal—not just a nice-to-have, but the cornerstone of a vibrant Christian life. Imagine waking up every day knowing you're not just anyone, but someone rooted in divine purpose. That's right, as followers of Christ, we've got a calling and a destiny. Our identity is grounded in the assurance that we are more than conquerors through Him who loved us. Not just conquerors, mind you, but "more than" conquerors (Rom. 8:37). What does that even mean? Well, buckle up for the journey of a lifetime.

Think of a conqueror and you might envision an ancient general leading his army to victory. However, as believers, our victory isn't marked by earthly triumphs. Instead, it's a spiritual reality anchored in what Jesus accomplished on the cross. Before you label this as too abstract, consider this—a conquering life in Christ kicks fatalism right out the door. God doesn't invite us to a do-nothing faith; He's molded us for action. There's no place for a passive mindset when you're wearing the armor of God. The Apostle Paul reminds us that we're "created in Christ Jesus for good works" (Eph. 2:10), which suggests that our identity should compel us to action—vibrant, dynamic, faith-driven action.

Now, pause for a moment and reflect on the transformative power of knowing who you are in Christ. This isn't about vanity or an inflated sense of self-worth. It's about recognizing the truth of our God-given identity and living from that reality. When you understand that you're adopted into the family of the King, it reshapes how you see every aspect of life. Challenges? They become opportunities. Setbacks? Merely setups for greater victories. Our identity in Christ ensures that no obstacle is too daunting when viewed through the lens of divine purpose and promise.

Let's get practical: knowing your identity in Christ informs your decisions, your relationships, and ultimately your legacy. Suddenly, life isn't about survival but abundant living. Don't think for a second that this is an easy-peasy journey. Nope, it demands courage, community, and faith. Biblical examples abound—from Gideon the reluctant warrior to Esther the courageous queen. Their stories teach us one crucial lesson: when you recognize your identity in God, you're equipped for divine mission.

In the coming chapters, we'll unpack how a passive mindset has no place in this grand narrative. For now, focus on embracing your identity with fresh zeal and excitement. Remember, God calls us by name, not by our failures or fears. It's time to step up and walk in the truth of who we are in Christ. Imbued with the Spirit and guided by the Word, you're empowered to live out this glorious calling. So go ahead—embrace the true you, anchored in faith and driven by love. After all, the world's weight is much lighter when carried on the shoulders of a conqueror destined for eternal victory.

Embracing the Role of a Conqueror

Picture a world where every believer steps into their true identity—armed with confidence, vigor, and the unwavering assurance that they are conquerors in Christ. Sounds unreal, right? Yet, this is exactly what we're called to be. The Book of Romans nudges us with a powerful reminder: "Yet in all these things we are more than conquerors through him that loved us" (Rom. 8:37). It's high time we shrug off any semblance of passivity and lean into our roles like a child rediscovering a superhero cape.

Now, I've met many who view Christianity as an endless cycle of kneeling in prayer, only to spring up with a feeling of uncertainty about their life mission. There's this notion that believers are destined to navigate life with the resignation of a sailboat in a dead calm. But we're called to more than just quiet endurance. In fact, our faith equips us to emulate the heroes of our favorite novels—where every page is packed with adventure, risks, and triumphs.

The first step in embracing the conqueror within is having an understanding of who you belong to. Knowing our identity in Christ isn't something to discover once and shelve like an old yearbook. Instead, it's a dynamic, transformative truth that should shape every aspect of our lives. Think of it this way: you're not merely part of a congregation. You're an essential member of God's kingdom, tasked with advancing His reign on Earth.

But how do you fully step into this role? Let's take a peek at the biblical narrative. We see countless instances where seemingly ordinary people achieved extraordinary feats because they embraced their God-given identity. Imagine when David walked onto the battlefield, a shepherd boy but in his heart, a king. He wasn't encumbered by stature or armor but armed with faith and determination. It's about switching your mindset from a "Why me?" to a "Why not me?" attitude.

To become conquerors, we must also toss out any spiritual lethargy that tells us it's all up to fate. A conqueror doesn't sit around waiting for victory; they strategize, plan, and move forward with confidence. As it says in Isaiah, "For I the Lord your God will hold your right hand, saying to you, Fear not; I will help you" (Isa. 41:13).

It's about knowing that you're not fighting alone. The Creator of the universe is literally cheering you on from the sidelines!

Our journey as conquerors is not meant to be a solitary venture. We thrive on the encouragement and experiences from our fellow warriors—our brothers and sisters in faith. Let me clarify, we might not exchange battle scars in the literal sense, but sharing victories and struggles fortifies us. How many stories have you read where the hero could only accomplish their task through the camaraderie and support of their community? It's exactly the same in our faith journeys.

Embracing the role of a conqueror doesn't require flawless strength or the luxury of a trouble-free life. Conquerors acknowledge hardships and weaknesses but do not allow them to dictate the final outcome. After all, the Apostle Paul reminds us, "I can do all things through Christ which strengthens me" (Phil. 4:13). It's that divine partnership, blending our efforts with God's boundless power, that makes the impossible possible.

So, go ahead, polish that imaginary armor and embrace the legacy of victory that is yours to claim. As you embark on this lifelong mission, recognize it's not merely about surviving the challenges but thriving and conquering them. Stand tall, secure in your identity, and let the world know that you are more than a conqueror, because you belong to Christ.

Biblical Foundations of Conquest

As we journey through understanding our identity in Christ, we find ourselves face-to-face with the notion of conquest—a term that can seem daunting at first. Conquest, defined in all its boldness, is not merely about territory or physical battles. Instead, it's about understanding and reclaiming our spiritual authority through Christ. The Bible, our guide, paints conquest not as a selfish power grab but as a divine commission to establish God's kingdom on earth.

Many might wonder, what business do we have, talking about conquest? Aren't Christians supposed to be meek and mild, turning the other cheek, as often quoted? While there is truth to humility and peace-making, the misinterpretation that Christians are called to live passive lives couldn't be further from what Scripture teaches. Just look at Joshua. As he led the Israelites into the Promised Land, God gave clear instructions: "Every place that the sole of your foot will tread upon, I have given to you, as I said to Moses" (Josh. 1:3). This wasn't a mission for the faint-hearted; it required bold faith and action.

The Biblical narrative is rich with examples of God's people engaged in acts of conquest—both physical and spiritual. These foundations remind us that faith is active and vibrant, not passive and stale. The story of David and Goliath, for instance, while thrilling to hear in Sunday School, is more than a boy and his sling. It is a tale of spiritual audacity and trust in God over physical might. David's confidence didn't rest in himself, but in the Lord of Hosts, whom he declared would deliver the giant into his hands (1 Sam. 17:46). This isn't just history but a template for how we confront spiritual giants today.

One of the greatest lessons from these narratives is that we, too, are called to be conquerors—not by our strength but through Him who strengthens us. The Apostle Paul, in his letter to the Romans, passionately asserts, "Yet, in all these things we are more than conquerors through him that loved us" (Rom. 8:37). What an invigorating reminder! We aren't mere survivors in the chaos of life; we are conquerors, a resounding testament to Christ's victory on the cross.

The battle isn't always against flesh and blood, as Paul illuminates in his letter to the Ephesians. Spiritual conquest means grappling with principalities, powers, and rulers of darkness (Eph. 6:12). Our weapons, then, are not carnal, but mighty in God for pulling down strongholds (2 Cor. 10:4). Armed with truth, righteousness, and the gospel, among others, we're equipped to make headway in advancing God's kingdom.

So, how do we swing into action on this foundation? It starts with a mindset shift—seeing ourselves not as timid bystanders but as active participants in God's plan. If in any way you're itching to equate conquest with aggressive dominion, consider Jesus. His triumph was embodied in humility and love. Our conquest today is about bringing peace, justice, and love where there is none, using the tools of faith, hope, and love.

The Book of Revelation offers a glimpse of our ultimate victory, promising that to those who overcome, Christ will grant to sit with Him on His throne (Rev. 3:21). This is not mere eschatological speculation; it's a call to action, a promise of what diligent, faith-filled living can achieve. It's assurance that our struggles in conquest aren't in vain and that there's joy unspeakable waiting at the finish line.

The Biblical foundations of conquest weave through the entirety of Scripture like a golden thread, challenging us to live bold, engaged lives. They remind us that while the path is tough, we are not alone. God has promised His presence, just as He assured Joshua when he trembled before the monumental task: "Be strong and of a good courage; do not be afraid, nor be dismayed: for the LORD your God is with you wherever you go" (Josh. 1:9).

Thus, in the face of trials, resistance, and the general hubbub of life, let's cast off any vestiges of passive living. As heirs with Christ, our identity is fortified by our calling—one steeped in the rich tradition of Biblical conquest. With a firm grasp on these foundations, let's march forward, bringing the light and love of God into every stride we take. After all, we've got the best Cheat Sheet around: the Word, a proven guide to navigating life's battlefield with gusto and grace.

Chapter 2:
Overcoming a Passive Mindset

Ever find yourself stuck in the proverbial waiting room of life, flipping through the outdated magazines of yesterday's spiritual joys? You're not alone. Many of us, convinced that the universe is on a slow train to heaven, sit back in our comfy recliners of complacency, popcorn in one hand, remote in the other. But is this really what God intends for us? In the words of Paul, "I press toward the goal for the prize of the upward call of God in Christ Jesus" (Phil. 3:14). There's a decisive call here to move, to press on, to refuse to sit still while life whizzes by.

Recognizing spiritual complacency is not about self-flagellation or sinking into a guilt pit. It's about a gentle wake-up call, like an alarm clock that nudges you out of a pleasant dream into the realm of purposeful living. We see this warning echoed throughout scripture, reminding us not to be "weary while doing good" (Gal. 6:9). But when faith becomes cozy and lukewarm, as Jesus warns the Laodiceans in Revelations, it's time we add a little holy spice to the mix. The world needs us, active and alive, not just as spectators but as players in the field of life.

Shaking off a passive mindset requires a proactive approach to spirituality. Let's not wait for God to sprinkle His providence on us like last-minute toppings on a sundae. Instead, it's about taking the initiative to actively seek His will, to involve ourselves in His grand narrative. It starts with the basics: scripture, prayer, and community.

Imagine it like a muscle that needs regular exercise. The more we flex it, the stronger it becomes. Perhaps it's time to embrace the challenges of faith with eagerness, much like David facing Goliath with nothing more than a slingshot and a prayer.

What's crucial here is recognizing that we're not alone. God doesn't expect us to sprint across the finish line by ourselves. In Philippians, we hear that "I can do all things through Christ who strengthens me" (Phil. 4:13). This isn't just a motivational quote for coffee mugs—it's the assurance to step out, assured of the backing from the Creator Himself.

Humor, too, can be a delightful companion on this serious journey. It allows us to view our challenges through a lighter lens, reminding us not to take ourselves too seriously whilst navigating these spiritual paths. A battering ram of joy can sometimes break through barriers far better than a woe-is-me approach. Laughter can be a thrumming heartbeat urging us forward, saying, "It's okay to stumble as long as you stand again."

So, as we unwrap this complex wrapping paper of spiritual passivity, perhaps it's worth asking ourselves: Where is God calling us to lean forward, to stretch out our tired arms, to reach for something beyond the now? Let's dare to be more than spectators. Let's lace up those metaphorical sneakers and get ready to run with patience the race set before us (Heb. 12:1). Life isn't meant to pass us by, and it's definitely not meant to be lived in passive resignation. We've got a purpose, and it's time to live it fearlessly.

Recognizing Spiritual Complacency

Once upon a time in the journey of faith, there's a dangerous rest area called spiritual complacency. It's a deceptively inviting spot on the Christian highway where the scenery is serene, but the soul's engine idles aimlessly. This isn't the bustling pit stop where you recharge with purpose; it's the kind of place where your spiritual ambition takes a nap on the hammock of comfort while the busyness of life plays a soothing lullaby.

Before you know it, you're living in the land of "good enough." Church attendance? Check. Daily devotional? Sort of. Prayers before meals? Absolutely. At first glance, it seems like you're cruising down the heavenly boulevard. Yet, in the heart's rearview mirror, you might notice the slight drift away from passionate pursuit toward passive contentment. Sadly, this is where many believers miss the compelling call to be conquerors, as Paul urges: "Yet, in all these things we are more than conquerors through him that loved us" (Rom. 8:37).

Let's admit it, recognizing spiritual complacency isn't as easy as spotting a mustard stain on your Sunday best. This sort of fog can sneak in when we're coasting on past achievements or resting on the laurels of our spiritual reputation. Remember that time when Peter, full of courage, insisted he'd never deny Jesus? Only to find himself warming his hands by a fire, complacency playing out in denial? Talk about a wake-up call with a rooster as the alarm clock (Matt. 26:34).

So, what are the signposts that tell us we're headed toward complacency? It starts with an indifference to spiritual growth—a lack of hunger for the things of God. You might find Bible verses resonating less, prayers turning mechanical, and worship becoming a plain old routine. These are not potholes; they're sinkholes into which one's spiritual vitality can plummet.

Don't be tempted to make your faith journey a passive drive-through. Complacency often plays handmaiden to routine. If your spiritual life looks like a never-ending reel of 'I've always done it this way,' it might be time to hit pause and reflect. Jesus didn't call us to 'ministry as usual' but to go the extra mile, turn the other cheek, and perhaps even love our neighbor by sharing with them the last piece of lasagna! Remember, if you always do what you have always done you will get what you have always gotten.

Breaking free from spiritual complacency doesn't require a prescription for a surprise lion's den experience—like Daniel's—but it may entail a diagnostic checkup of the heart. What propels your faith journey—is it the spirit of obligation or the joy of the Lord? Because Nehemiah reminds us, "the joy of the Lord is your strength" (Neh. 8:10), and nobody wants to ride a spiritual rollercoaster without proper safety bars!

Humor aside, recognizing the subtle drift toward spiritual complacency is essential for a vibrant Christian walk. Engage the tools God has given: His word, fellowship, and the transformative work of the Holy Spirit. Sometimes the Holy Spirit nudges with whispers and at other times with a cosmic two-by-four, urging believers to stay out of spiritual autopilot. As in Hebrews, "Let us hold fast the confession of our faith without wavering" (Heb. 10:23).

Think of a roaring fire, vibrant and intense. Now picture that same blaze dimming, its flames reduced to embers. Spiritual passion works similarly; it requires diligent attention to stay ablaze. Regular logs of Scripture, prayer, fellowship, and worship are necessary to keep the light from flickering. Without them, complacency wins, and the fire becomes a mere flicker.

Ultimately, spiritual complacency is an invitation to revisit our first love (Rev. 2:4) and rekindle the flame. It asks us to swap a passive mindset for one that's constantly seeking, knocking, and asking. After all, if we seek Him passionately, He assures us, "For everyone that asks receives; and he who seeks finds" (Matt. 7:8). Spiritual complacency is the adversary of adventure; let's vow to choose the divine quest instead.

As you venture onward, take this chapter as a friendly nudge—a clarion call to step off the moving walkway of passivity. Dive deeper into the uncharted waters of faith where God's promises shine brighter. Keep your eyes on the prize, and remember, even as we walk through valleys of complacency, our Shepherd offers guidance every step of the way (Ps. 23:4). Let's stride forward with renewed fervor, courageously casting aside complacency for the dynamic, fulfilling life that God designed for us.

Strategies for Living Proactively

Imagine that your life is like a ship sailing through the unpredictable ocean of time, endowed with the untapped power of God's promises. But here's the kicker: you've been cruising on autopilot, and it's about time you grab the wheel with both hands. As Christians, we're not only called to a life of faith but one that's brimming with proactive engagement. So, let's dive into the vibrant strategies that can transform any passive mindset into one that teems with purpose, zeal, and dynamism.

First up, getting clear on *who* is truly in charge is pivotal. It's like when God called Moses from a burning bush and effectively said, "I've got a task for you, my friend" (Exodus 3:10). We need to recognize that this proactive lifestyle isn't about moving under our own steam. Rather, it's rooted in seeking divine guidance and letting that shape our actions. The trick is that God won't hijack our schedule; we have to invite Him to direct it. Remember, "For you were once darkness, but now are you are light in the Lord: walk as children of light" (Eph. 5:8). As children of light, our path should be one illuminated by intentional choices.

Let's talk about setting meaningful goals—a concept that might sound cliché but stick with me here. Goals grounded in our Christian values set the pace and direction for our journey. They focus our efforts and create boundaries that prevent distractions. Consider Nehemiah, who rebuilt the walls of Jerusalem despite opposition because he was laser-focused on his God-given task (Nehemiah 6:3). He demonstrated that proactive living requires both a clear vision and tenacity forged in faith.

We also can't ignore the role of courage in living proactively. Joshua, successor to Moses, was encouraged repeatedly to be strong and courageous as he led the Israelites into the Promised Land (Josh. 1:9). Courage gets us to make the first move, to voice that idea, or to face that challenge we've been dodging. It comes down to believing that God's power within us is greater than any obstacle.

Embracing flexibility is just as important. Living proactively while rigidly clinging to our plans can send us into rough waters. Think of the apostle Paul, whose missionary journeys were often rerouted by the Holy Spirit. At times, he was redirected to a completely different area than what he intended (Acts 16:6-10). Being adaptable allows God to steer us toward His best for our lives, even if it doesn't align with our original blueprints.

Next, consider the value of action. Lack of action sidelines us into a passive existence. Remember what James said, "Thus also faith by itself, if it does not have works, is dead." (James 2:17). We can't just sit around expecting spiritual lightning bolts to ignite our circumstances. Action paired with faith is like jumping into God's river of grace and allowing Him to carry us forward.

The essence of proactive living also involves being spiritually vigilant. Life can throw curveballs—think of Jesus instructing His disciples to watch and pray so that they wouldn't fall into temptation (Matt. 26:41). Vigilance keeps us alert, helping us to notice opportunities that are often disguised as interruptions or challenges. It's in these moments that we can harness God's wisdom to navigate our path ahead.

Mentorship shouldn't be overlooked, either. Seeking the guidance of those who are seasoned in faith brings invaluable insights and accountability. Paul mentored Timothy, equipping him with the wisdom needed for his ministry (1 Tim. 1:2). Investing time with mentors can propel us forward and keep us grounded as we embark on our proactive pursuits.

Lastly, we should remain rooted in gratitude. Being thankful doesn't just compel us to keep going; it keeps our headspace wired toward recognizing abundant blessings. "In everything give thanks: for this is the will of God in Christ Jesus for you" (1 Thess. 5:18). A mindset of gratitude sees challenges not as interruptions but as divine opportunities for growth.

Ultimately, to live proactively as Christians is to actively participate in the divine narrative God has orchestrated. It means grabbing hold of the here and now, knowing that our destiny is secured in Christ, while we courageously plant seeds of faith in every moment. Step off the sidelines—redirect your ship with purpose under the banner of "more than conquerors," for that is your destiny.

Chapter 3:
Advancing the Kingdom of God

In this rallying march forward, Christians are called not merely to be spectators but active participants in the grand play of divine purpose. The Bible thunders with the call for believers to be daring with their faith, like David charging at Goliath, armed not just with stones but the unwavering belief that "the battle is the Lord's" (1 Sam. 17:47). Advancing God's kingdom isn't about retiring to a cozy pew every Sunday, hoping for change like waiting for a bus that never comes. It's about rolling up your sleeves and engaging in spiritual warfare, not with swords, but with love, prayer, and the conviction that you're more than conquerors through Him who loves us (Rom. 8:37). Our mission, while daunting, is gloriously guided by the assurance that with God, all things are possible (Matt. 19:26). It's a vibrant dance of faith—sometimes stumbling, often leaping, always trusting—that carries Heaven's rhythm down onto earthly streets. So grab hold of your calling, laugh in the face of fear, and step boldly into the fray, knowing that every act of faith advances this eternal kingdom, inching heaven towards earth, one God-breathed act at a time.

Taking Initiative in Faith

When you think about "taking initiative in faith," imagine you're standing at the edge of a cliff with a bungee cord securely fastened around you. It's that exhilarating leap of trust into the unknown, anchored by the belief that God's got you. Every act of initiative in faith is a small leap, an active decision to step into the promises and purposes God has laid out. It's not passive or timid but a bold declaration that you're all in, ready to engage fully in the adventure called faith.

Now, let's break that down. Faith isn't just stagnant belief; it's dynamic, alive, and constantly moving. The Apostle James puts it succinctly when he says, "Faith without works is dead" (James 2:26). Active faith calls for more than just a Sunday morning nod to the sermon. It's about rolling up your sleeves and getting to work, driven by a conviction that what God has promised, He is also able to perform.

Picture Noah. Building an ark must have seemed absurd at times—constructing a titanic vessel on dry ground while neighbors wagged their heads in bemusement. Yet Noah demonstrated initiative in faith by acting on a divine directive long before the first drop of rain. His faith was the hammer driving the nails, each act of building another testimony to trusting God. Noah didn't wait to see the swell of clouds to start gathering wood. He laid board upon board in faith's obedience, reminded once again of a promise he hadn't physically seen but was assured of in his spirit.

But where do you begin? How do you shift from dreaming to doing, especially when it feels like you're stuck in the allocated boundaries of doubt? Start by acknowledging that God has wired you—yes, you—for action. Ephesians 2:10 tells us, "For we are his workmanship, created in Christ Jesus for good works, which God has prepared beforehand that we should walk in them." Here, the canvas for our life's masterpiece isn't finely painted by our hesitations but by divine acts of courageous faith.

Think of the disciples when Jesus called them. Peter, James, and John dropped their fishing nets to follow Him. They didn't draft a pros and cons list or check their schedules for availability. They heeded a call that tugged at their spirits with compelling urgency. Their initiative wasn't just in quitting their day jobs; it was embarking on a journey greater than themselves. It meant participating in a work that was eternal, a Kingdom that's unshakable. They took initiative by answering the call to follow and, ultimately, fishing for souls rather than sardines.

The momentum of initiative opens doors to arenas where faith muscles can flex. Consider David before he was king. He could have easily remained the young shepherd boy ensconced safely in fields. Instead, he stood before Goliath, his senses alive with divine confidence. David's initiative wasn't blind folly; it was cultivated through practicing faith as he defended his flock from lions and bears. He didn't wait for someone else to step up. In 1 Samuel 17, he declares, "This day will the Lord deliver you into my hand" (1 Sam. 17:46). His courage to confront Goliath came from seeing past the giant to the victory God had already promised.

Modern-day Goliaths vary, but the principle holds. When you seize spiritual opportunities instead of shrinking back, it's in those moments God shows up in spectacular ways. You choose to lead a Bible study at work, visit the sick, or even go on a mission trip. It's the decision to serve selflessly or speak a word of encouragement just when someone needs it that strengthens your faith muscles.

Importantly, taking initiative in faith doesn't mean going it alone. It requires a community of believers who spur each other on toward love and good deeds (Heb. 10:24). Surround yourself with those whose faith journeys inspire you to jump further and dream bigger. Fellowship involves accountability—sometimes you need a nudge when sidelines comfort you more than the field.

Consider Mary, the mother of Jesus. When the angel Gabriel announced the most unimaginable news, Mary said, "Behold the maidservant of the Lord; Let it be to me according to your word" (Luke 1:38). Her initiative was implicit in her submission and acceptance, paving the path for salvation history. There's a profound lesson here: initiative can also mean saying "yes" to God's unexpected assignments, trusting in His timing and wisdom.

If faith is the engine, then initiative is the wheels turning, guiding it toward the promises God has on the horizon. It's the ongoing decision to engage mind, body, and spirit in the kingdom affairs and trust the Holy Spirit to lead. After all, "for it is God who works in you both to will and to do for his good pleasure" (Phil. 2:13). Your role is continuous action, allowing God to work through your available heart and hands.

How empowering it is to think: the same Spirit that raised Jesus from the dead lives within us, animating our faith to spring into action! Every prayer, ministry effort, or seemingly insignificant act of faith contributes to our calling. Remember, no step taken in the pursuit of God's kingdom is futile.

So, what are the clouds on your horizon where God's whisper beckons? Look beyond the natural eyes. Dare to take the first step— even if it's into the unknown. God never demands us to see the end of the road, only the next step in faith. Like Isaiah, let the anthem echo, "Here am I; send me" (Isa. 6:8).

Engaging in Spiritual Warfare

We've all read those epic battle stories in the Bible. You know, the ones where David slings a rock, Goliath falls, and the Israelites have an unlikely victory party. Or when Joshua and his crew march around Jericho so many times you start to wonder if they're stuck in some kind of prayer-driven treadmill race. While these tales can leave us wide-eyed and inspired, they're not just ancient bedtime stories. They're vivid snapshots of what it means to engage in spiritual warfare today.

But before you rush out to the nearest slingshot store, let's talk about what "spiritual warfare" really means. It's not about donning armor or clanging swords. It's about recognizing that we're in the middle of a battle that's both unseen and very real. Paul didn't mince words when he said, "For we wrestle not against flesh and blood, but against principalities, against powers, against the rulers of the darkness of this world, against spiritual wickedness in high places" (Eph. 6:12). This isn't a Hollywood action flick—it's the truth of our Christian walk.

Now, don't panic. This isn't a call to draft a battle plan like a twelve-step program. Instead, it's an invitation to be part of a divine mission, advancing the Kingdom of God on Earth. Our battlefield might not look like the plains of the Philistines. It might look more like a disagreement at home, a challenge at work, or a shadow of doubt in our heart. Recognizing these moments as arenas of spiritual warfare flips the script, allowing us to tackle them with Heaven's perspective.

Humor me for a second. Imagine if every little squabble with your sibling or disagreement at work was actually an opportunity for spiritual victory. Wild thought, right? Sure, slaying dragons sounds more dramatic, but the truth is, most battles are won in the quiet moments. They're won in prayer, in biting our tongues when our ego says, "fire away," or when we choose love over judgement. These choices are our armor, our invisible slingshots, and our declarations of faith.

The Bible never leaves us hanging. In Ephesians 6, Paul gets practical about our battle gear. He talks shields, helmets, belts and, interestingly enough, footwear. "And your feet shod with the preparation of the gospel of peace" (Eph. 6:15). Have you ever thought of peace and the gospel as shoes? They ground us, make us ready to move, to stand firm, or go the extra mile. So, lace them up!

Let's have a bit of motivation here. Think of a time you felt God urging you to take a step of faith. Maybe it was a nudge to speak to someone about Christ or to act in kindness where others turned a blind eye. In those moments, we engage in spiritual warfare by advancing God's Kingdom through tiny, faith-filled decisions. Each act, a small stone launched against a giant.

And who could forget about tactics? Like any successful campaign, engaging in spiritual warfare demands a strategy. Daniel didn't just resist Babylonian culture; he doubled down on prayer, even when the lions were waiting. Nehemiah tackled obstacles with fervent prayer and practical action (Neh. 4:9). These spiritual warriors knew when to fall to their knees and when to stand up and build.

Remember the scene with Daniel locked in the lions' den, yet cool as a cucumber? That's the power of confidence in faith. It's not about ignoring danger but knowing who's by your side. God has equipped us with righteousness, faith, and salvation as spiritual armor (Eph. 6:14-17). It's His power, not ours, that sees us through.

Now, a touch of wit—God's advisory can't be found in a slick marketing brochure. It's packed in Scripture and prayer. Joshua didn't win battles by a fluke. He absorbed God's instructions like a kid with a sponge, "This book of the law shall not depart from your mouth; but you shall meditate on it day and night" (Josh. 1:8). It's our roadmap too.

"Pray without ceasing" (1 Thess. 5:17), Paul advises. Now, don't worry—no need to neglect life's joys for a monastic vow. It's about adopting a constant conversation with God in our hearts, tuning into His guidance in every step we take. It's this continual prayerful posture that makes us spiritual warriors in our daily lives.

And what of the enemy's tactics? Yes, there'll be times when doubts and fears knock on the door like unwanted guests. When they do, look them squarely in the eye and stand on the truth. Jesus Himself set the pattern in the wilderness. When tempted, He spoke, "It is written…" (Matt. 4:4). Knowing Scripture isn't just for Bible trivia night; it's our weaponry, our shield, our guide.

But let's not go it alone. The Bible is full of warriors, but none of them fought solitary battles. Paul mentions, "Praying always with all prayer and supplication in the Spirit, being watchful to this end with all perseverance and supplication for all the saints" (Eph. 6:18). Community is born not just of fellowship, but of strategic partnerships in prayer and shared mission. We need each other, whether to stand shoulder to shoulder or to give someone a nudge toward the front line.

In all this, don't forget joy. Spiritual warfare might sound grim, but there's a joy that transcends the fray. Isaiah captured it: "Therefore with joy you will draw water from the wells of salvation" (Isa. 12:3). Joy isn't fluff; it's the deep, sustaining emotion that says, 'Victory is in God's hands, and I'm aligning myself with His power.'

The Kingdom of God advances, step by joyous step, through believers determined to engage in spiritual warfare with confidence, courage, and God-given authority. Our mission, should we choose to accept it, is not to strike fear but to inspire faith, to illuminate the darkness, and to let God's light shine. After all, "The battle is the Lord's" (1 Sam. 17:47).

So, steel your heart, lift your spirits, and march onwards. In this arena, each prayer, each act of faith, advances the Kingdom more than we could ever imagine. Boldly, let's play our part in the grand story, aware of the power that walks before us, beside us, and within us, ready to claim victories designed long before we were born.

Chapter 4:
Empowered by the Holy Spirit

The notion of empowerment can seem like a billboard on life's highway, constantly passed and seldom truly understood. In the Christian context, empowerment by the Holy Spirit transforms this concept from a motivational slogan into a living, breathing experience. It's like having spiritual superpowers—a divine boost to our everyday struggles and triumphs. We aren't just onlookers in life's grand theater; we're the actors, directors, and even the stagehands, energized by the Holy Spirit to participate actively in God's plan.

Without the Holy Spirit, trying to live a Christian life can feel a lot like pushing a boulder uphill. But let's face it—most of us aren't Herculean by nature. Thankfully, as believers, we've been promised a Helper. In the Book of Acts, we see the disciples transformed from uncertain, timid followers to bold proclaimers right after Pentecost. It was a dramatic makeover, and no wardrobe or makeup change was required; it was all internal, through the Holy Spirit's power. "But you shall receive power when the Holy Spirit has come upon you" (Acts 1:8). This promise isn't just for the disciples; it's for us too.

One might wonder, what does this empowerment look like in everyday life? Think of it as the difference between clumsy stumbling and confident dancing. It's not always about grand gestures; often, the Holy Spirit guides in whispers rather than shouts. A nudge to call a friend in need, a sudden burst of courage to face a daunting task, or a calming peace in the storm—these are the subtle yet profound workings of the Holy Spirit. But when the Spirit moves, watch out! Hearts can change, mountains can move, and even a bit of humor can sneak into the most somber situations. "Now the Lord is the Spirit: and where the Spirit of the Lord is, there is liberty" (2 Corinthians 3:17).

In this empowered state, the Bible introduces us to the fruits of the Spirit. Love, joy, peace, long-suffering, kindness, goodness, faithfulness, gentleness, and self-control aren't just nice characteristics to have—they're the vital signs of Spirit-led living. It's as if God decided to give us an internal checklist. And, as with any good produce, these fruits need to be cultivated. The Holy Spirit waters these seeds within us every day, enabling us to become who we were always meant to be.

To tap into this divine guidance, we need to listen—not just hear, but truly listen—and follow where the Spirit leads. Here's the hook: it might lead us out of our comfort zones. But isn't that where the magic happens? We're not talking pulling a rabbit out of a hat here; we're referring to kingdom magic, where lives are transformed, and God's love is made manifest. As the Book of Romans reminds us, "For as many as are led by the Spirit of God, they are the sons of God" (Romans 8:14). It is why the Father gave us the Comforter, the Holy Spirit, because he knew we would be uncomfortable at times.

In the end, being empowered by the Holy Spirit is akin to turning the lights on in a dim room. Suddenly, everything is illuminated with purpose and potential. So, let the Spirit guide you to dance through life with joy and courage, knowing that your empowerment comes from the greatest source of all—a divine Helper who's always by your side.

Gifts and Fruits of the Spirit

Without a doubt, embarking on the journey empowered by the Holy Spirit is like getting a VIP pass to the greatest adventure of them all. Picture this: a delectable buffet that doesn't just fill you with temporary satisfaction but nourishes your soul. The gifts and fruits of the Spirit, dear friends, are such delights. They're not just available for the super-spiritual elite; they're divinely sanctioned rights of all who claim identity in Christ, and they're here to transform you from a passive spectator into an active participant in God's divine drama.

The Holy Spirit is like the ultimate multi-tool—think Swiss Army knife for the soul. In 1 Corinthians 12, Paul describes a grand array of gifts bestowed upon believers. These gifts, ranging from wisdom and knowledge to healing and prophecy, are like your spiritual toolkit, ready to equip you for every situation life throws at you. Paul writes, "But the manifestation of the Spirit is given to each one for the profit of all" (1 Cor. 12:7). These gifts aren't just for show; they're meant for Christ's work on Earth. You've got skills, and the Holy Spirit's got surprises to enhance them.

Now, it's tempting to want to pick and choose our favorite gifts like we're at a candy store. But the Spirit distributes them as He sees fit, a divine matchmaker parachuting perfect gifts at just the right moments. So, you're not just a pedestrian Christian; you're handpicked for greatness! Whether you're speaking in tongues or administering healing, it's about working together in unity, like a symphony where each instrument has its moment to shine.

Yet, what's the point of having gifts if they aren't seasoned with the right spirit? That's where the fruits of the Spirit come into play. In Galatians 5:22-23, Paul lists these fruits as love, joy, peace, long-suffering, kindness, goodness, faithfulness, gentleness, and self-control. Unlike the gifts, which are given individually, these fruits are attributes that every believer should exhibit. They are not just fleeting virtues that you experience occasionally; they're the hallmark of a life deeply rooted in the Spirit.

The fruits of the Spirit aren't about putting on a show of moral heroics. They remind me of perseverance in a long race. The fruits manifest when you're in traffic and someone cuts you off, and instead of honking like a maniac, you choose peace and patience. These fruits serve as a testimony of your journey toward spiritual maturity. In a world obsessed with immediate gratification, cultivating these fruits requires intentionality and continual surrender to the Spirit's gentle guidance.

If the gifts are the tools, the fruits are the manner in which we wield those tools. Picture a master craftsman who not only has the finest equipment but also the self-control to use it skilfully. In the same way, bearing the fruits of the Spirit enables each of us to use our gifts effectively. Love becomes the lens through which prophecy is proclaimed, gentleness shapes the delivery of encouragement, and patience becomes the steady hand guiding healing. This is God's master plan: a harmonious life of gifts and fruits working together.

Throughout the New Testament, we see believers who became conduits for God's power through their spiritual gifts. The apostles, despite their initial failings and fears, grew into the giants of faith we celebrate today. Peter, once impulsive and impetuous, became a foundational pillar for the early church. His gift of teaching and leadership, tempered with the fruits of patience and humility, advanced the Kingdom in ways unthinkable before Pentecost. It wasn't him, but the Spirit through him that achieved miracles.

Having gifts and manifesting fruits isn't about attaining spiritual bragging rights. It's about becoming an authentic ambassador of Christ's compassion and grace. The world isn't short on people who know how to call attention to their own accolades. But it desperately needs those who are willing to selflessly serve with nothing more than the quiet power of Spirit-driven action. Paul wisely advises, "Let all things be done decently and in order" (1 Cor. 14:40), reminding us to strike a balance and walk the line of grace.

Let's not overlook the incredible role that community plays in nurturing these gifts and fruits. The church is a fertile ground where budding gifts receive water and light, where infant fruits learn to mature. Imagine a grand tapestry made of vibrant threads of diverse gifts intricately tied together with the fruits of the Spirit. In the fellowship of believers, we find accountability, encouragement, and opportunities for the gifts to flourish.

The beauty of gifts and fruits lies in their reciprocity—they're meant to be shared. Like any good harvest, these spiritual attributes not only nourish you but those around you. In using your gifts, the church becomes edified, and when you bear the fruits of the Spirit, you make room for the world to taste God's goodness. It's a cycle of giving and receiving, all within the glorious dance orchestrated by the Holy Spirit.

The journey of faith isn't a passive, fate-driven trek. It's a vigorous, Spirit-empowered adventure full of twists and turns. The gifts and fruits of the Spirit are your faithful companions, ensuring you're well-equipped and well-mannered for the path ahead. So go ahead, embrace them. Exercise them. Let the Spirit guide you, and you'll soon find that the Christian life is not only fulfilling but highly impactful. Indeed, "you shall receive power, when the Holy Spirit has come upon you" (Acts 1:8), and with that power, you are not just a conqueror—you are more than a conqueror.

Listening to and Following Divine Guidance

Listening to and following divine guidance can sometimes feel like trying to catch the wind—it's elusive but vitally important. After all, if we're aiming to live empowered by the Holy Spirit, hearing His guidance should be as routine as our morning coffee. The Holy Spirit is described as a Counselor ("John 14:26"), guiding us into all truth and whispering heavenly wisdom we might not think up on our own.

How, then, do we become more attuned to this divine guidance? Much like tuning a radio to the right frequency, it's about fine-tuning our spiritual senses. The first step is intentional quieting of the chaos around us. Our world is a cacophony of notifications, reminders, and distractions. The Psalmist reminds us, "Be still, and know that I am God" ("Psalm 46:10"). In this stillness, we become more receptive to the Holy Spirit's gentle nudges.

But listening isn't a passive activity; it's an act of engagement. The practice involves not only listening but being willing to follow where that guidance leads—even if it's into uncharted waters. Consider Abraham—a veteran at following divine directions. Called to leave everything familiar and go to a land he'd never seen, Abraham didn't respond with a laundry list of concerns. He moved. Empowerment comes when our willingness to obey matches His willingness to guide.

Following divine guidance requires discernment, balancing between the noisy clamors of the world and the subtle whispers of the Spirit. This discernment is sharpened through Godly wisdom and scriptural alignment. Scripture serves as our compass. If the guidance contradicts the Bible, it's safe to say it's not coming from the Holy Spirit. Remember, "All scripture is given by inspiration of God, and is profitable for doctrine, for reproof, for correction, for instruction in righteousness" ("2 Tim. 3:16"). The more we embed ourselves in Scripture, the clearer this discernment becomes.

It's not unusual for divine guidance to nudge us out of our comfort zones. Sometimes it's a small whisper to speak kindness to a stranger or set aside time for prayer. Other times, it's the unmistakable call to make bold, life-altering decisions. In any case, the objective remains the same: transformation into the likeness of Christ and the nature of the Father and the advancement of God's kingdom on Earth.

Ironically, God's guidance often leads us into uncertainty, where control is merely a fallacy. This is where faith kicks in as the supernatural glue holding our wobbly human knees steady. "For we walk by faith, not by sight" ("2 Cor. 5:7"). Divine guidance might not always make logical sense, but that's the beauty and mystery of faith-led living. Just ask the Israelites marching around Jericho—logic didn't fit into God's strategy, yet the walls came tumbling down.

Moreover, divine guidance isn't just about monumental life decisions. It's in the everyday choices, the mundane and repetitive acts of obedience that might seem insignificant. It's sharing lunch with a colleague who's having a rough day, or feeling compelled to check in on a friend. These small actions can have ripples of eternity when led by divine guidance.

We must also be vigilant against the pitfalls of doubt. Often, we question whether we've truly heard from God or if it's just our wishful thinking. A litmus test for divine guidance is the peace it brings—a peace that might defy circumstances. "And the peace of God, which surpasses all understanding, will guard your hearts and minds through Christ Jesus" ("Phil. 4:7"). His guidance aligns with His character and fruits of the Spirit, one of which is peace.

Listening and following the Holy Spirit's guidance fuels a life of purpose and fullness. Imagine life as an intricate dance, with the Holy Spirit leading and us responding to His every move. This dance shapes our character, aligns us with our divine destiny, and nudges us ever closer to Christ's likeness. Isn't that the ultimate goal?

The key to continuous empowerment by the Holy Spirit lies in our willingness to listen and follow. It's a partnership, an ongoing dialogue, and a relationship that can revolutionize how we live, love, and lead.

Conquest

Jesus assures us that, "my sheep hear my voice, and I know them, and they follow me" ("John 10:27"). Our task is to remain as diligent and loyal as sheep, trusting the Shepherd and following His voice.

As we cultivate this relationship, we're invited into the grand narrative that God is writing—one of restoration and redemption. We become pivotal actors in His divine play, each scene bringing us closer to the transformation that stands at the heart of our faith journey. So, let's make room for the Holy Spirit's guidance, make it a daily pursuit, and embrace the wondrous adventure of being empowered from above.

The dance of guidance and response holds the power to transform our everyday experiences into testimonies of faith and conviction. As we tune our hearts to listen and muster the courage to act, let us envision a life painted with divine strokes—where each step is a part of His masterpiece.

Chapter 5:
Building a Strong Prayer Life

Picture prayer not as a mere religious duty but as the lifeline that keeps your spiritual heart beating. It's a powerful tool in a Christian's arsenal, akin to a direct hotline to Heaven, where you can dial God anytime—no hold music, guaranteed. As prayer becomes more consistent, like daily bread for the soul, it nourishes and forms the backbone of a robust Christian life. The Apostle Paul challenges us, "Pray without ceasing" (1 Thess. 5:17), nudging us to foster an unbreakable connection with God throughout our day. But let's keep it real: not every prayer session will feel like the heavens are parting. Sometimes, it's simply about showing up, an act of faith itself, and trusting that God is in the whispers as much as in the shouts. The beauty lies in persistence and creativity, in praying as naturally as breathing, whether you're inspired in a quiet corner or mid-chaos at the kitchen sink. So, strap on those prayer boots, get comfortable in your sacred space, and let your prayer journey be as dynamic and diverse as God made you to be.

The Importance of Consistent Prayer

Remember David and Goliath? That classic story where a young shepherd armed with nothing but a sling and some stones took down a giant powerhouse. It's not just a tale of improbable victory; it's an illustration of what happens when prayer becomes an integral part of life. This isn't a sporadic, "help me pass this test" sort of plea—it's consistent prayer, the steady heartbeat of a life lived in communion with God. So why's it important? Because without it, you'd be trying to conquer your giants without the Creator of the universe backing you up. Imagine wandering into a battle with no game plan.

In the fast-paced lives we lead, marked by to-do lists as long as the day, prayer can sometimes seem like a daunting task to squeeze in. Yet, it's in these moments of quiet reflection and connection with God that we find the strength to go from surviving to thriving. James artfully reminds us, "Draw near to God, and he will draw near to you" (*Jas. 4:8*). Consistent prayer is how you draw near, making it less of a formal occasion and more of a continuous conversation.

Think of it like watering a plant. Miss a day, and you might still see green leaves, but skip it for long enough, and you'll notice the withering. Your spiritual life is no different. Consistent prayer acts as a spiritual watering can, nurturing growth, and grounding you in faith. The regular dialogue with God fortifies your roots, enabling you to stand tall in life's fierce windstorms. It is not just about asking for things but aligning your will with His.

Let's be clear: Consistently praying isn't about a rigid schedule of kneeling for ten minutes every night before bed. While routines are helpful, consistency in prayer can take many forms. It might be whispering a prayer while waiting for the morning coffee to brew or offering thanks during a lunch break. How about shopping for groceries and expressing gratitude for each item? The apostle Paul wasn't kidding when he wrote, "Pray without ceasing" (*1 Thess. 5:17*); it's a lifestyle, not a checklist item.

Consistency builds a habit, and habits shape who we are. It's easy to think about building character as a grand task reserved for retreats or Bible study marathons, but the truth is more subtle. The character is sculpted in the dailiness of life. It's in moments like a well-timed prayer that you gradually become more attuned to God's heart and begin to see your life—and the world—through His eyes.

The strength of consistent prayer lies in its ability to transform your mindset. It's the spiritual nudge that dares you to step off the sidelines and enter the game. Like Joshua was encouraged by God to embrace the truth, "Have not I commanded you? Be strong and of good courage" (*Josh. 1:9*). With a prayer life that's consistent, you become equipped to face trials head-on with unwavering faith and the assurance that God is with you every step of the way.

Prayer is often seen as our lifeline in times of trouble. But it's crucial to remember that it's not just a lifeline—it's a lifeblood. Committing to consistent prayer also aligns our lives more closely with God's wishes, turning us into capable conduits of His blessings and power. When used like this, prayer becomes less about asking and more about aligning; it's creative collaboration with the divine.

While it's tempting to box it up as a solitary exercise, consistent prayer thrives in community. Shared prayers in fellowship provide unity and strength like the early Christians who "all continued with one accord in prayer and supplication" (*Acts 1:14*). It's about knowing you aren't a lone ranger in your spiritual journey but part of a bigger narrative where your story intertwines with others.

It's like charging your phone. Just as an uncharged phone loses its usability, a faith without consistent prayer runs the risk of power drain. You might get distracted by a glittering new app or a call that demands your attention, but sooner or later, you'll need to plug back in. And when life throws a curveball, having that steady connection means you're immediately tapping into wisdom, peace, and strength far beyond your own.

Moreover, consistent prayer builds resilience. One day the sun's shining, you're hitting green lights, and you've got a free upgrade to first-class. Next, the skies open up, traffic's terrible, and your coffee graciously finds its way onto your shirt. Through it all, prayer solidifies the fortress of your soul. You become less reactive to your circumstances and more responsive to God's calling. It's this resilience that transforms adversity into opportunity and setbacks into setups for divine action.

Prayer consistently also opens a treasure trove of gratitude. The longer you engage with God through prayer, the more aware you become of His active presence in your life. It shifts your perspective, allowing you to see His fingerprints on your daily blessings. That newfound appreciation naturally spills over into every area, infusing your everyday routine with joy and contentment.

So here it is, all wrapped up: The importance of consistent prayer isn't merely about discipline or desire. It's about transformation. It's about showing up each day, trusting that even if you don't have the words, books, or verses ready, your heart still speaks volumes. Through prayer, you align with His love and power to become conquerors in your own right. Let this be an invitation not just to conquer your own spiritual giants but also to inspire others to do the same.

Effective Prayer Strategies

Alright, so let's delve into the nitty-gritty of developing effective prayer strategies. Because let's face it, sometimes our prayer life feels like throwing darts in the dark and hoping something hits the target. But a strong prayer life isn't about hitting the bullseye by chance; it's about intentionally aiming with confidence and precision. Now, that's where strategy comes into play.

Firstly, let's talk about the prayer schedule. Setting aside a specific time for prayer might seem like a chore at first, like scheduling a dentist appointment or gym session. Yet, it's the consistency that builds strength. Daniel had a habit of praying three times a day (Dan. 6:10)— and this man ended up in a lions' den without losing his cool. Coincidence? I think not. God honored his dedication.

Now, for those who thrive on a bit of structure, consider incorporating various forms of prayer into your routine. You might structure your prayer time with a blend like ACTS: Adoration, Confession, Thanksgiving, and Supplication. Adoration is recognizing God's majesty, Confession is laying down our burdens, Thanksgiving involves showing gratitude, and Supplication is asking for what we need. Mixing up these forms prevents prayer from becoming a monotonous ritual.

Secondly, let's embrace the power of the Word. Prayer is significantly more potent when it's grounded in Scripture. Ever noticed how Jesus countered temptation in the wilderness not with personal defense mechanisms but with scripture itself? "It is written" is quite the comeback strategy (Matt. 4:4). When prayer is intertwined with scripture, it aligns you with God's promises, which adds extra layers of faith and fervency to your petitions.

Also, never underestimate the significance of the heart's posture in prayer. It's not just about the words we speak but the attitude with which we approach our Creator. Humility is key, because, after all, "God resists the proud, but gives grace to the humble" (James 4:6). Consider how the tax collector beat his breast in repentance, and in doing so found favor before God (Luke 18:13-14).

Let's sprinkle in some humor with another approach—prayer partners. Now, don't underestimate the awkward misplaced laughs and shared glances. But really, Jesus said it himself: "Where two or three are gathered together in my name, I am there in the midst of them" (Matt. 18:20). By joining forces in prayer, not only do you build community, but you also amplify the power of your petitions.

Ever tried writing your prayers down? A prayer journal might just be the tool you didn't know you needed. Whether it's pouring out your heart or jotting down specific requests, it serves as a tangible reminder of God's faithfulness. Weeks or months later, you can flip through and see how many prayers God has answered and in what unique ways He's worked in your life.

But strategic prayer doesn't just look inward. It's a call to look outward and intercede for others. Praying for others shifts the focus from ourselves and aligns us with God's mandate to love our neighbors. Intercession sharpens our empathy and broadens our perspective, often inspiring action.

Another powerful strategy is using the physical senses in prayer. Picture yourself in the scenario you're praying about or even go on a "prayer walk." As you walk through your neighborhood, community, or even in nature, allow the sights and sounds to inform your prayers. These tangible reminders often spark new insights and inspirations.

We can't forget the importance of gratitude in our prayer life, and not just during Thanksgiving in November. Starting and ending prayers with thanks, regardless of current circumstances, shifts the focus onto what God has done and can do. Remember what Paul said, "In every thing give thanks: for this is the will of God in Christ Jesus concerning you" (1 Thess. 5:18). Gratitude alters perspective.

Finally, let's embrace the spontaneity of prayer. Structured times are crucial, yet shooting up a quick prayer in a moment of need or gratitude, whether you're in a crowded subway or before a job interview, emboldens the idea of a constant connection with God. As 1 Thessalonians 5:17 succinctly states, "Pray without ceasing."

In conclusion, while these strategies provide various paths to a solid prayer life, remember there's no one-size-fits-all approach. Just like conversations with friends differ, creativity in prayer can lead to a richer and more fulfilled connection with God. So, mix and match, adapt and explore, but most importantly, stay committed. With persistence and a dash of faith, your prayer strategies will not just conquer the mundane but will empower you to live victoriously—a true conqueror in Christ.

Chapter 6:
The Role of Community and Fellowship

Continuing our journey of transformation, we arrive at the vibrant intersection of community and fellowship. Here, we're reminded that we're not lone warriors on a barren battlefield but members of a dynamic, interconnected body. In the hustle of life's tempest, we draw strength from one another, sharpening and uplifting as iron sharpens iron (Prov. 27:17). Embracing this unity, we channel the Apostle Paul's exhortation to "bear one another's burdens, and so fulfill the law of Christ" (Gal. 6:2). With humor and joy, we build relationships that are more than fleeting interactions; they're soul-deep connections. These bonds become our safety nets and springboards, propelling us forward. Indeed, the church isn't just a place—it's a living, breathing fellowship of believers where no conqueror journeys alone. Let us plow onward, cultivating a community rooted in love and powered by faith, knowing that, together, we reflect the dazzling mosaic that is the body of Christ (1 Cor. 12:27), each piece essential and divinely placed.

Strength in Unity

Picture this: a lone soldier standing on the battlefield, fully armored yet overwhelmed by the encroaching enemy. Compare that image with a well-formed battalion, moving in perfect harmony, shields interlocked, protecting and propelling one another forward. The latter, isn't it, is an unmistakable force to be reckoned with? This is what community within the Body of Christ is meant to be. A singular power emerging, not from solitary might, but from an unyielding collective strength. "For where two or three are gathered together in my name, I am there in the midst of them" (Matt. 18:20).

Unity in community is like a divine symphony, each one of us playing our part, diverse instruments contributing to a beautiful, harmonious whole. The Apostle Paul often beautifully illustrated this concept using the analogy of the body—many members, one body. In his letters to the Corinthians, he reminds us that "the body is not one member, but many" (1 Cor. 12:14). Consider how seamlessly our own bodies work: the hands, feet, eyes, and ears, all functioning in unity to achieve a single purpose. Even the smallest part plays an integral role. The Christian community is no different; every individual, with unique gifts and talents, is essential.

What do these spiritual platoons look like in practice, you might ask? Well, they're the glue that holds us together, the cushioning that softens the blows of life's inevitable challenges. Imagine a church community forming a network of support, where meals are brought to new parents and prayers lift up the sick. It's Mabel checking in on her elderly neighbor from church, or John setting aside time to mentor the youth group, reminding each young soul that they belong. This isn't just nice-to-have; it's a necessity. In Galatians, we are told to "bear one another's burdens and so fulfil the law of Christ" (Gal. 6:2). Community is God's tangible extension of His love and care.

In large part, the strength of unity also comes from shared accountability. It's about having someone call you out when you've strayed slightly off path and equally, someone cheering you on when you're running the race well. A good friend can remind you of who you are when you've momentarily forgotten, echoing that age-old wisdom found in Proverbs: "Iron sharpens iron; so, a man sharpens the countenance of his friend" (Prov. 27:17). This sharpening isn't always comfortable, but necessary. The ability to lovingly correct and be corrected builds resilience in faith and character.

Naturally, unity doesn't mean the absence of conflict. Indeed, conflict can be the refining fire that strengthens the bonds of community. When approached with a heart aligned with Christ's teaching, disagreements can lead to greater understanding and growth. Practice the wisdom of Ephesians, where it says, "Let all bitterness, wrath, anger, clamor, and evil speaking be put away from you, with all malice: And be kind to one another, tenderhearted, forgiving one another, even as God for Christ forgave you" (Eph. 4:31-32). Forgiveness is the balm that heals wounds and knits hearts closer together.

Now imagine how this unity transforms our mission as conquerors in faith. Envision advancing the Kingdom of God not as isolated warriors but as a cohesive unit, each one inspiring the next—this is evangelism at its most effective. There is no opting out, no sideline Christianity, everyone is a vital part of the Great Commission. "Two are better than one, because they have a good reward for their labor. For if they fall, one will lift up his companion" (Eccl. 4:9-10).

More than anything, community provides a real-world demonstration of God's love and kingdom, a vibrant picture that often speaks louder than words. Authentic relationships grounded in the gospel are infectious. They don't just attract others but transform them. Observing such unity can be like witnessing a lighthouse on a stormy night—a beacon of hope and guidance for those who feel adrift.

The world can often be an isolating place. Screens separate us, and sometimes busyness blinds us to the needs of others. In a society that often values individual success over collective well-being, the church has the extraordinary opportunity to be countercultural—to model a Christ-centered community where each person's story and struggle is shared. Jesus Himself prayed fervently for our unity: "That they all may be one; as you, Father, are in me, and I in you, that they also may be one in us" (John 17:21). There's hardly a more important mission.

Thus, engaging in community isn't simply obligatory, it's transformational. It's where you replenish your spiritual tank and where you add fuel to someone else's fire. This is not just about Sunday morning fellowship or mid-week Bible studies, it's a call to intertwine our lives daily, beyond the walls of a church building. Whether it's helping your neighbor or inviting someone for a meal, these seemingly small acts strengthen the fabric of God's family.

So, start small but start somewhere. Turn up, speak truth, share burdens, celebrate victories, and infuse grace into any gathering of believers. Remember, unity does not require sameness, but a shared vision towards a collective glorification of God's kingdom. When our hearts beat in sync, we find ourselves living out Christ's commandment "that you love one another; as I have loved you, that you also love one another" (John 13:34), becoming witnesses not only in word but in deed.

Let us be the embodiment of that battalion on the battlefield, a community so united that no power of hell or scheme of man can sever the bond of unity forged in love and galvanized by faith. By drawing strength from one another, we mirror the love of Christ and stride forward together, equipped for any battle that a conqueror might face.

Building Supportive Christian Relationships

In the divine strategy of life, where God has placed us like dots on the grand tapestry, the intersection of our lives with others isn't merely incidental—it's intentional. Relationships are designed by our Creator to be rich, nourishing, and immensely supportive. The Bible says, "Iron sharps iron; so a man sharpens the countenance of his friend" (Prov. 27:17). This forging process doesn't happen in isolation. It's the clang of lives meeting together, each sharpening the other in Christ's love.

Forming supportive relationships within a Christian community might seem like a task for the extroverts of the world, but guess what? It's a calling for everyone. God's blueprint for the church is community-based because it reflects His own triune nature: a harmonious relationship within Himself. This communal design challenges us to step out of the shadows of solitude and into the light of fellowship. Our task is to weave a network of connections that echo Christ's love, offering unity, strength, and courage for each journey we face as conquerors.

The early church perfectly embodies this principle of support through community. Acts tells us that the believers "continued daily with one accord in the temple, and breaking bread from house to house, they ate their food with gladness and simplicity of heart" (Acts 2:46). This was not just about nourishment for the body but for the soul, too. Their unity was their strength, enabling them to stand unwavering in times of persecution, much like the camaraderie of soldiers fighting alongside each other in a battlefield.

Let's be honest here—the idea of prioritizing relationships isn't always appealing. When life feels like an ever-churning hamster wheel, it can feel counterproductive to invest time in others. Yet, these relationships are precisely what God uses to infuse our lives with balance and enrichment. A well-timed word from a friend can illuminate our darkest days. As we're reminded, "A friend loves at all times, and a brother is born for adversity" (Prov. 17:17). These friendships are God-given lifelines woven into our stories.

But what makes a relationship truly supportive and rooted in Christian love? It's about depth rather than breadth. Quality over quantity, as they say. We're not talking about superficial engagements here but about relationships girded with prayer, honesty, and gracious love. It's about having the courage to listen more than you speak, to empathize rather than advise hastily, and to gently steer when someone's veering off the path without becoming an unsolicited navigator of their life.

We've got to keep in mind that strong Christian relationships are built by God-fueled intentionality. This might mean stepping outside of our comfort zones to invite someone for coffee or expressing heartfelt concerns instead of mere conversations about the weather. We take the risk of being vulnerable—showing the cracks in our own armor, thus allowing others to come alongside us with Christ-like compassion and wisdom.

On this road of building supportive relationships, accountability partnerships can be powerful. Here's where we dive deep guarding each other's hearts and spurring one another on in our walk with Christ. The Apostle Paul had his Barnabas, a companion that offered encouragement while also challenging him to grow. "Two are better than one, because they have a good reward for their labor. For if they fall, one will lift up his companion" (Eccl. 4:9-10). Accountability aids us in keeping focus, whether on spiritual disciplines or God-driven missions.

Communal worship and shared faith experiences also play a critical role in fostering these relationships. There's something spiritually rhythmic about joining voices in praise, our hearts beating in unity. It's where individual praise melds into communal worship, reaffirming that we're a part of something bigger than ourselves. Our faith experiences become binding threads that connect us, sprinkling seeds of testimony within us that grow into a shared narrative of God's abundant grace.

Let's remember that building supportive Christian relationships isn't just an inward-focused endeavor. It's as much about reaching out as it is about looking in. Every interaction we have with believers and non-believers alike is an opportunity to share the love of Christ. When we embody Jesus's commandment to "love your neighbor as yourself" (Matt. 22:39), our community becomes a vibrant testament to God's boundless love. Our actions, rooted in love and service, become living parables written on the hearts of everyone we encounter.

When difficulties arise—as they inevitably will—supportive relationships become the safety net beneath us. Life's trials can become triumphs with the encouragement and prayers of those who lead us back to the Father time and time again. It's the shoulders we cry on, the ears that listen without judgment, and the hands that reach out to pull us up. Together, we discover that even the darkest valleys are navigable.

In cultivating these relationships, patience and forgiveness are key. Offenses may come, and misunderstandings happen, but it's grace that bridges the divide. Grace seeks not just to endure mistakes but to transform and renew relationships. Jesus set the ultimate example of sacrificial love and forgiveness, and it's by His example we learn to look beyond our imperfections and extend the grace we've freely received.

Through laughter, through tears, through heartening conversations and sometimes challenging confrontations, supportive Christian relationships are God's chosen tool for chiseling us into the image of Christ. When we walk this life not as lone wanderers but as part of God's collective, we embrace the full breadth of what it means to belong to the family of God, conquering not just for victory's sake but for loves.

In the end, the essence of building supportive Christian relationships lies in the radical and relentless pursuit of love, as Paul so eloquently wrote, "And now abide faith, hope, love, these three; but the greatest of these is love" (1 Cor. 13:13). It's love that binds us, equips us, and ultimately propels us into the world as vibrant testimonies of the Gospel's truth. Let's walk this road together, hand in hand, sharpening and being sharpened, for God's glory and our collective growth.

Chapter 7:
Navigating Challenges and Trials

Life's a bit like a rollercoaster; it's thrilling and terrifying all at once, but we've got a secret weapon: faith. When trials come—and they will—we're not just passive passengers! We're called to be intrepid adventurers guided by God's unwavering truth. Paul once said, "I can do all things through Christ which strengthens me" (Phil. 4:13). Now, that's a rallying cry! Whether it's dealing with a tough boss or grappling with inner fears, these trials are less about what happens to us and more about how we respond. Like David slinging stones, we meet adversity head-on, armed with prayer and the Word. Maintaining faith means keeping ourselves grounded, even when the storm rages. Jesus calmed the seas, after all! Hard times aren't a reason to falter; they're an invitation to grow, a divine opportunity to strengthen our spiritual muscles. Embrace each trial as a testament to the strength of our faith and His unending love.

Finding Strength in Adversity

Life's challenges often come in waves, don't they? Just when you've managed to catch your breath from one, another comes rolling in. It's like being in an endless arcade game of 'whack-a-mole" but with fewer stuffed animal prizes at the end. Yet, as Christians, we're not left alone to face these obstacles; we're gifted with the incredible opportunity to find strength in adversity.

Embracing adversity might sound as thrilling as hugging a cactus, but in the grand scheme of things, it's part of our divine blueprint.

Throughout the Bible, we see heroes of faith like Joseph, Esther, and Paul all navigating turbulent waters with profound resilience. Let's not forget Paul, who remarked, "I can do all things through Christ who strengths me" (Phil. 4:13). He's not speaking from a beach chair under a palm tree, sipping a piña colada. No, Paul was in chains, facing the harsh realities of prison life, a testament to finding strength where others see only defeat.

Consider this: adversity is somewhat of a spiritual gym. Sure, there's no membership fee unless you count the sweat of perseverance and the occasional teardrop. Just like physical muscles grow by lifting ever-increasing weights, our spiritual muscles develop with each trial. But how do we lift this proverbial weight when the burdens seem insurmountable? We start by shifting our perspective.

Shift your gaze upwards—not just metaphorically, but spiritually. Remember Peter stepping out of the boat onto water? It's not the turbulent sea that defines the moment, but Peter's faith and his focus on Jesus. The lesson here is simple yet profound; when our eyes are fixed on the storm, we sink. When they're fixed on Christ, we walk. The storm may rage, but our faith doesn't have to falter if we keep our vision locked on Him.

That's where humor plays its part, a surprising tool in handling hardships. Humor can be an armor, shrouding us against despair. Even Abraham and Sarah chuckled at the impossible promise of a child in their old age. It's as if they said to their skeptics, "Just wait and see what God can do!" That's finding levity amidst life-defining struggles—knowing joy is both our strength and our God-given right (Neh. 8:10).

However, channeling strength through adversity isn't just about an optimistic outlook. It's about our foundation. Jesus illustrated this beautifully in His parable of the wise and foolish builders. A house built on rock withstands storms, while the one on sand crumbles (Matt. 7:24-27). Our "rock" is our faith, built on the Word of God, prayer, the Holy Spirit's guidance, and strengthening our community bonds.

Throughout the trials, remember that adversity is not rejection; it's God's redirection. Look at Jonah, reluctantly redirected from fleeing to fortuitously reviving a city. At times, adversity plunges us into a belly-of-the-whale moment—a transformative dark pause which allows for reflection and recalibration.

As you engage with life's adversities, consider adopting some battle-tested strategies. Prayers, folks—a potent, two-way conversation with the Creator. It's therapeutic, empowering, and sometimes even wordless; "Likewise the Spirit also helps our weaknesses. For we do not know what we should pray for as we ought: but the Spirit himself makes intercession for us with groanings which cannot be uttered" (Rom. 8:26).

In closing, it's imperative to recognize the strength we garner in adversity isn't from sheer willpower or stubborn tenacity alone. It's intricately tied to the Divine. As iron sharpens iron, so too are we refined and made resilient through life's fiery trials. Let's face adversity not with passive resignation but with an assurance—a faith that sings through the storm, that laughs in the face of defeat, and that celebrates victory already secured through our Savior.

Maintaining Faith Through Difficulties

Life has an uncanny way of throwing curveballs when we least expect them—financial struggles, health crises, relational breakdowns—each one a potential Goliath to our unsuspecting David. It can feel like a relentless boxing match, and if we're not careful, our faith might get knocked out cold. But as Christians, maintaining faith through difficulties isn't just a line in a self-help book—it's a calling. It's an opportunity to stand in the furnace of life's trials and declare, like

Shadrach, Meshach, and Abednego, that our God will walk with us through the fire (Dan. 3:25).

That sounds noble, but how do we actually do it? For starters, let's get real about the fact that faith isn't a fluffy cushion to soften life's blows. It's more like a sturdy shield. Remember how Paul describes faith as a shield in the armor of God (Eph. 6:16)? This isn't just poetic language; it's strategic. Faith is what enables us to trust in God's promises even when the scenes of our lives look like they've been hijacked by a particularly dastardly episode of "Murphy's Law." If you're teetering on the brink of despair, it's time to wield your shield with renewed vigor.

But wielding faith isn't a solo sport. It's more of a team relay, where communal encouragement plays a huge role. Imagine what would've happened if Moses had tried to part the Red Sea without the support of his people behind him. Fellowship acts as a buoy to lift our spirits when we're caught in the floodwaters of trouble. God designed us for community, and there is strength and revival in shared struggles and victories, much like when Paul found camaraderie in the early Church amidst persecution (Acts 14:27).

Yet, in moments of solitude during our trials, it's crucial to anchor ourselves in God's character. We might be tempted to suspect God's silence as indifference, but remember, even when Jesus was quiet before Pilate, He was fulfilling His greatest purpose (John 19:9-11). Our trials aren't a stage for God to exit; rather, they're the backdrop for Him to work in our inner selves. When trust seems like a leap too far, we can ground ourselves in the history and truth of God's unchanging nature—that He who began a good work in us will carry it on to completion (Phil. 1:6).

Now, let's talk about perseverance. The book of James tells us that the trying of our faith works patience (James 1:3). It's like baking bread—the yeast of trials makes our faith rise, though it requires the heat of adversity. We can't skip this process if we wish to grow spiritually mature. Want proof? Look no further than Joseph, who languished in prison years before becoming Pharoah's right-hand man. His faith didn't develop in spite of difficulties, but rather through them.

Humor, surprisingly, can be one of the most divine gifts in adversity. While it might sound counterintuitive, laughter amid trials is not about diminishing the gravity of our circumstances but finding joy and lightness despite them. If joy is a fruit of the Spirit (Gal. 5:22), then humor is like a nudge from the Holy Spirit to not take our earthly dilemmas too gravely. God Himself has a sense of humor, evident in the spectacle of a tiny shepherd boy bringing down a giant. It's this joy that becomes our strength in the face of life's rocky roads (Neh. 8:10).

Finally, as we maintain our faith through difficulties, the Bible becomes our navigational chart—guiding, correcting, and comforting us. It's where we encounter countless stories of perseverance and victory. If you've ever felt like shaking your fists at the sky in confusion and anger, take solace in knowing you're in good company. Job, lamenting in his ashes, never got his direct answers, but he did encounter God in a profound way (Job 38-42). These narratives fuel our faith, assuring us that we, too, can emerge from trials with a richer, deeper, and more resilient faith.

In conclusion, maintaining faith through challenges isn't about having all the answers or living trial-free. It's about embracing the journey with resilience, community, biblical truths, and maybe a dash of humor. As we move through the ebb and flow of life's trials, may we echo the words of Paul, holding fast to his declaration: "I can do all things through Christ who strengthens me" (Phil. 4:13). Our faith doesn't shield us from life's waves, but it certainly empowers us to surf them, sometimes clumsily, sometimes gracefully, but always with the hope of eternity propelling us forward.

Chapter 8:
The Power of Testimony

As we march forward in our journey, let's dive into the power of testimony—it's more than just sharing a story. It's lighting a beacon of hope, showing others that our challenges aren't without purpose. When we speak of what God has done in our lives, we're cementing the truth that "faith is the substance of things hoped for, the evidence of things not seen" (Heb. 11:1). Our stories can transform doubt into belief, hesitation into action. And while we might think we're simply recounting personal experiences, we're building bridges of understanding, encouraging others to see God's fingerprints across their own journey. Every testimony is an act of defiance against passivity. Remember, faith is not a museum piece; it lives, breathes, and yes, surprises. So let's not keep silent. Instead, let our words spark faith in others, because who knows? Your story might just be the roadmap someone needs to navigate their own stormy seas. In the grand tapestry of life, these accounts become threads of courage, boldly defying the darkness with light, echoing Paul when he said, "I have fought a good fight, I have finished my course, I have kept the faith" (2 Tim. 4:7). Go ahead, let your voice become a testament of triumph.

Sharing Personal Faith Experiences

There's something inherently powerful about standing up and sharing your personal faith story. It's like exposing your inner self, revealing the journey that brought you closer to God. Sure, it might seem daunting at first, like bungee jumping without really knowing if the cord is securely fastened. But faith, as unpredictable as it seems, often catches us in surprising ways, much like that reassuring snap of the cord when we freefall into the unknown.

Sharing your testimony isn't just about narrating a neatly wrapped story where every question has an answer and every problem is neatly resolved. In fact, it's often the jagged edges, the unfinished edges of our stories, that speak the loudest. Paul's experience on the road to Damascus was anything but neat and tidy ("Acts 9:1-19"). It was raw, emotional, and transformative. And it's those very elements that make personal testimonies connect with others, striking chords and evoking empathy.

Think about it – every time you share with a friend or stranger tales from your walk with God, you're offering something unique and irreplaceable. Your story is an intricate tapestry of faith, woven with experiences that no one else has lived through quite like you have. In fact, there's a marvelous kind of empowerment that arises when you share your testimony. It's like shouting from a mountaintop, declaring the wondrous works of God in your life, and inspiring others along the way.

The art of sharing these faith experiences lies not just in the message, but in the delivery. Remember Peter, standing up to address the multitudes at Pentecost? ("Acts 2:14-41") His heart and courage were undeniable, and the impact of his words was far-reaching. Much like Peter, when you're open and genuine, authenticity shines through and becomes a conduit for the Holy Spirit's work.

Testimonies allow others to see firsthand what's possible with God. They say, "Hey, if this person has experienced the grace of God in such a profound way, perhaps I can too." Faith shared is faith amplified. It is a beacon of hope, a gentle nudge to someone who might be wobbling on the edge of doubt. It is crucial not to stray into a territory where one's testimony shifts from being a story of God's glory to merely showcasing personal accolades.

Moreover, when we venture to share, it becomes a two-way street. We testify, and in doing so, others are encouraged to reciprocate with their own stories. It's this dynamic interplay that enriches the community of believers, spurring each other on in the race marked out for us ("Heb. 12:1").

Now, let's sprinkle a bit of humor into this serious business – because who says faith experiences have to be somber all the time? When you're threading stories from your life, don't hold back the quirky and funny bits. Maybe there was that time you ended up in the wrong church because of a GPS error but found yourself moved to tears by the sermon. Or perhaps, during a prayer meeting, your phone suddenly blasted an unexpected rendition of "Eye of the Tiger" – seemingly perfect for a moment of divine inspiration.

Allow these moments of levity to shine. They remind us that God is present in all moments of life, not just the solemn ones. Life, after all, is a tapestry of varied experiences – some somber, some spirited, some absolutely riotous. And within this tapestry, God weaves His divine purpose, urging us to craft our testimonies in relatable, human terms.

Don't underestimate the potential of your story. Remember the woman at the well, who after a single encounter with Jesus, went back to her town and convinced many to meet Him ("John 4:28-30"). All she did was tell her story. Sometimes, it's not about having all the answers, but about pointing others towards the source of all answers – Christ.

Finally, find inspiration through Biblical narratives. Share moments where you felt like Jonah, running the opposite direction only to be tugged back by divine intervention ("Jonah 1:3"). Recall times where you endured trials like Job, yet found redemption and restoration in the end ("Job 42:10"). These powerful parallels remind us that we're part of a continuum, and our stories are a small, yet significant, piece in the grander narrative God is weaving.

So, embrace the courage to share your personal faith experiences. Infuse them with humor and delight, affirm their power in testimony with authenticity. For every word spoken, you're not only reinforcing your own faith but shining a light for others on their paths. After all, in this shared journey of faith, sometimes the most profound testimonies come from ordinary steps taken in extraordinary belief. Let's keep walking, sharing, and inspiring one another in this great adventure with God.

Encouraging Others Through Storytelling

The power of a story lies not just in its telling, but in its ability to connect hearts, ignite passions, and transform stagnant mindsets. Jesus knew this when He spoke in parables, rich tales woven with heavenly truths and earthy wisdom. But how do these stories, personal as they are varied, inspire others to kick off the shackles of passivity and embrace a triumphant Christian life? There's a world of influence waiting in our shared experiences, for these testimonies have the potential to propel believers into active faith—one fellowship to another.

Stories are the bridges across the chasm of indifference. Consider the narrative of David and Goliath. It is a grand story of conquest against the odds, but it also carries a deeply personal assurance: the impossible becomes possible when God strengthens the heart. When we share our own stories of divine intervention, we plant seeds of faith in weary fields. It's like saying, "If God can move mountains for me, then He can surely do it for you."

Take, for instance, those moments when sharing our own tales of triumph over fear or weakness. These are more than mere anecdotes;

they become a road map for others. They say, "You are not alone. I've walked this path, and here's what I've learned." Instantly, the listener is no longer a passive onlooker in their own life. They've got a blueprint for active participation in God's promises.

Let's not underestimate the impact of humor in these stories. The Bible tells us that "a merry heart does good like a medicine" (Prov. 17:22). A little laughter can open doors to deeper understanding. When we laugh together, barriers fall. Laughter creates a human connection, an equal footing on the sometimes-rocky road of faith. Humor turns the lights on in those dim corners where serious subjects might otherwise reside, bringing them into the glorious light of day.

Besides humor, biblical reference adds to our tales. We connect the profound with the personal when we thread scripture through our narratives. Begin with a familiar verse, perhaps "I can do all things through Christ who strengthens me" (Phil. 4:13). Allow that varnished truth to resonate like a chord, then entwine it with a snippet from your life's song.

Sometimes, storytelling requires a bit of vulnerability, opening up those areas we'd rather keep hidden. The Apostle Paul was never one to shy away from revealing his struggles. He wrote about his "thorn in the flesh" (2 Cor. 12:7), giving us all a safe space to admit our own battles. When we reveal weaknesses, it's a call to gather folklore from the margins of our spiritual walk, bringing it right into the living room of God's family.

But it's not just the apostles or biblical giants whose stories matter. Every believer's story is a thread in the grand tapestry of God's Kingdom. Look around in your community—stories are everywhere. Remember the elderly woman in church who shares how God carried her through the loss of a spouse, or the young man who struggled with addiction but found redemption in Christ. Their testimonies stir up something profound: hope and encouragement.

Conquest

What's more, storytelling can be a training ground for greater works of faith. Think of it as an informal internship for living out the Gospel. As you articulate your encounters with Christ, the narrative strengthens your own faith, girding you with new energy for future spiritual battles.

And don't forget the power of a well-timed story to catalyze change. Imagine sitting in a small group and sharing how you moved from financial despair to blessing by tithing faithfully. Suddenly, the others start seeing God's provision in their own financial stresses. Your story becomes a seed of change, urging growth and a mindset shift from scarcity to abundance.

In the end, storytelling in the Christian community is more than just a form of entertainment or mere surface-level chatter. It's an act of spiritual warfare against complacency. It disputes the pervasive myth that we're merely passive spectators in the divine play, reminding us we're called to be conquerors through Christ.

So, unfurl those stories, dear friends, with a spirit of boldness and a truth-filled heart. Layer them with scripture, sprinkle them with laughter, and share them with vulnerability. Root them in God's promises, and you'll leave the listeners not just entertained, but energized and equipped for their journey. Let's keep crafting and sharing these testimonies—not just for our own sakes, but to spur each other on toward love and good deeds (Heb. 10:24). With every tale told, the Kingdom of God advances a little further.

Chapter 9:
Living Faith in Action

Where mere belief falters, action takes flight, establishing faith as a powerful driving force that transcends passive observation. Picture a world where faith isn't confined to pews and Sunday best, but is released into the wild, where it intersects daily life and impacts society. Does faith have meaning if it doesn't influence our deeds? James got it right when he said, "faith without works is dead" (James 2:26). This doesn't mean acquiring a messiah complex; it's about allowing your beliefs to weave through your day-to-day actions. Imagine every small act of kindness as a modern-day miracle, every call to justice as an echo of divine purpose. To live your faith is to engage in the ongoing symphony of service, where each note played through deeds and words creates a melody that resonates with the core teachings of Christianity. The Apostle Paul boasted humility when he exhorted us to "run with patience the race that is set before us" (Hebrews 12:1), emphasizing the journey over the destination. So lace up those spiritual running shoes and let your faith propel you into action, knowing that every step ignites a spark of hope in a world desperately in need of it.

Demonstrating Faith Through Works

As we journey through our Christian lives, many of us grapple with the question: "How do we truly live out our faith?" It's easy to say we have faith, but demonstrating it through action is where the rubber meets the road—it's not just about talking the talk but walking the walk. James puts it bluntly: "Faith without works is dead" (James 2:26). Harsh, maybe, but it's the kind of honesty we need when it comes to understanding the depths of authentic Christian living.

Think of faith as a trusty car sitting in the driveway. It's got a glorious paint job, a powerful engine, and all the bells and whistles that scream potential. But without turning on that ignition, without pressing on the gas, it's just sitting there looking pretty. It's through works—through action—that faith revs up, engages, and moves forward.

Now, let's peel back the layers and get to the heart of the matter. Demonstrating faith through works isn't about trying to earn God's approval or ticking off a divine checklist. Jesus already took care of the salvation bit on the cross. The truth is, our works spring forth from the gratitude and love we have for the Lord. Consider Peter's words when he instructs us to "add to your faith virtue," which serves as a reminder that faith is just the beginning of a transformed life (2 Peter 1:5).

Remember the story of the Good Samaritan? It's not just a tale designed to make us feel warm and fuzzy. It's a radical call to action. Here's a guy who didn't just stroll by and murmur a prayer for the injured fellow. He stopped, got his hands dirty, and provided help—no questions asked. That's the kind of faith-in-action that leaves a legacy and changes lives.

Some might counter with, "But I'm doing okay just relying on faith. Isn't that enough?" While it's true that faith is at the core of who we are as believers, it's important to recognize that works are the natural outflow of a living faith. As Paul declares in Ephesians, "For we are his workmanship, created in Christ Jesus for good works, which God prepared beforehand that we should walk in them" (Ephesians 2:10). Good works are part and parcel of our spiritual DNA.

Now, if you're wondering how your faith can move mountains—or at least make a dent—it doesn't mean you need to uproot your life and become a missionary in the farthest corners of the globe. It might be as simple as lending a listening ear to a friend in need, volunteering at your local shelter, or supporting a single mom who's overwhelmed. Whether big or small, these acts matter enormously in the grand tapestry of God's kingdom!

Here's something to chew on: faith in action also means leaning into God's promises and taking bold steps in areas He's nudging you toward. Recall how Abraham obeyed and went, even though he didn't know where he was going (Hebrews 11:8). He waved goodbye to comfort, choosing instead to embrace a journey into the unknown. That takes guts, doesn't it?

As believers, we should never underestimate the ripple effect of our actions. One simple act of kindness can ignite a chain reaction of grace and love that reverberates through lifetimes. Who knows? Your faith-filled work could be the catalyst for someone else to discover or deepen their relationship with Christ. Wouldn't that be something?

In our pursuit of demonstrating faith through works, let's keep a sense of humor and lightheartedness. After all, God is a God of joy, and sometimes a good laugh can be just as holy as a reverent prayer. We aren't called to be somber saints, forever burdened by the weight of duty. Instead, we're called into joyous action—liberated by the love and grace of God.

So, how do we continue this journey without burning out or losing focus? Look to the Holy Spirit, our trusted friend and guide. As Paul assures in Galatians, the Spirit gives us love, joy, and peace, among other fruits, to help us in this endeavor (Galatians 5:22-23). When we align ourselves with the Spirit, we'll find the strength and wisdom required to engage fully in the work God has prepared for us.

Conquest

In summation, let your faith be vibrant, alive, and tangible through your actions. We have been chosen for such a time as this, to shine like beacons of hope in a world that sometimes feels overcast. While the journey may have its bumps, the reward of seeing faith at work, transforming both ourselves and those around us, is immeasurable.

Instead of becoming complacent, let's be the kind of Christians who fearlessly roll up our sleeves and get to work. It's our privilege, responsibility, and calling. At the end of the day, demonstrating faith through works isn't just another chapter in our lives; it is the epicenter of living faith in action.

Impacting Society as a Believer

When we think about making an impact on society, it's easy to picture a massive movement or a revolution. But consider the tiny mustard seed that eventually becomes a great tree ("Matt. 13:31-32"). Sometimes, big change starts with small steps. As believers, every action we take flows from our faith and has the potential to ripple out into the world, touching lives in ways we might never fully understand. We're ambassadors of Christ here on Earth, and with that comes a responsibility that's both a challenge and a joy.

Let's face it: the world can be a challenging place. Each day we wake up to a society that's often at odds with our beliefs and values. Yet within these very challenges lie infinite opportunities for impact. The apostle Paul reminds us that we are not to be "conformed to this world" but to be "transformed by the renewing of your mind" ("Rom. 12:2"). This transformation is both personal and communal; it starts within us and extends outward, influencing the communities and societies around us.

One way to impact society is through acts of kindness. Have you ever been on the receiving end of unexpected kindness? It's transformative, right? In the same way, our actions can have a profound impact on others. Every kind act, no matter how small, can be a seed that grows into faith and hope in someone else's life. "Let your light so shine before men, that they may see your good works, and glorify your Father which is in heaven" ("Matt. 5:16"). This verse isn't just an invitation; it's a call to action.

Yet, impacting society isn't just about individual actions. It involves engaging in the larger narratives at play in our world. This means standing up for justice, speaking truth into situations filled with falsehoods, and serving those who are marginalized or disadvantaged. Remember, Jesus spent His time among sinners and tax collectors, not in the palaces with kings. He fed the hungry, healed the sick, and welcomed the outcasts. His life was a living testament to the power of love and truth.

But let's not romanticize this—it isn't always easy. Taking such stands can be grueling and may even isolate you from the mainstream. Yet, look no further than Daniel in Babylon, maintaining his faith in a foreign land. He exemplified how a steadfast spirit can move the heart of kings and change nations. We, too, can affect the structures of our world by holding onto our convictions while engaging with people around us in a loving and respectful manner.

It's a mistake to think our faith is just a personal matter—it is deeply public. Our faith should inform how we vote, where we spend our money, how we treat our neighbors, and even how we engage in our professions. "But be doers of the word, and not hearers only, deceiving yourselves" ("James 1:22"). This Scripture reminds us of the broader implications of living out our faith: it requires action.

Consider the early church and how it impacted society. Often, they did not have the backing of political power or wealth. What they had was a community deeply rooted in love, bound by faith, and invested in sharing the Gospel. Their profound sense of mission enabled them to change the world, one relationship at a time. Their example challenges us to ask, what can we achieve with the resources God has already given us?

In living our faith out loud, we're called to use our unique gifts and callings. Not everyone will be a missionary or pastor, but all roles are important. Whether you're an artist, engineer, teacher, or stay-at-home parent, you're equipped to be salt and light precisely where you are. Our society needs believers who radiate love, humility, and wisdom, bringing a touch of Jesus' unconditional love into secular spaces.

Engage in genuine dialogue with others and showcase empathy. Sometimes it's the conversations over coffee with a co-worker or the patient listening ear extended to a neighbor that sows the seeds of faith. While the goal isn't to convert every interaction into a sermon, being genuinely interested and loving towards others makes a strong impact. Remember, "By this all will know that you are my disciples, if you have love for one another" ("John 13:35"). Love is the ultimate identifier and impact-maker in society.

Imagine a society where every believer acts as a conduit of God's love and righteousness. Nuanced decisions, selfless acts, and transformative dialogue shape the societal landscape. In every corner of the world, there's an opportunity to let the values of the Kingdom shine through. Every decision we make and action we take can echo eternity.

The task is daunting, but the rewards—eternal. As we press onward to impact society, we should remember that we're not alone. The Holy Spirit empowers us, the community of believers supports us, and the love of Christ motivates us. Let us go forth and live intentionally, transforming the world one small act of faith at a time. Amen.

Chapter 10:
Managing Spiritual and Emotional Health

So, you've conquered jungles of complacency and scaled the mountains of faith, but now it's time to tackle your own heart and mind—a territory just as wild and wondrous. Managing spiritual and emotional health isn't merely about surviving, but thriving with the assurance given in Philippians 4:7, "And the peace of God, which surpasses all understanding, will guard your hearts and minds through Christ Jesus." Whether dealing with spiritual exhaustion or the relentless hum of modern life, it's crucial to balance faith with self-care, understanding that even Jesus withdrew to pray and rest (Mark 6:31). Don't mistake this for inaction; consider it recalibration for the soul. Just like a well-tuned instrument, your spirit needs regular maintenance to resonate well. With a little humor and a lot of divine wisdom, recognize the signs of burnout before you're running on spiritual fumes. Remember, even warriors of faith unwind, so your strength can be renewed like an eagle's (Isaiah 40:31).

Balancing Faith Life with Self-Care

You know that feeling when a rubber band is stretched just a little too far? It starts to strain and fray, losing its elasticity. Our spiritual lives can feel much the same when stretched between our commitments in faith and the vital necessity of self-care. We're called to be conquerors, not casualties of the spiritual tug-of-war.

Conquest

Balancing faith life with self-care might sound like a modern wellness trend, but it's more than that—it's biblical. Our bodies are temples of the Holy Spirit, as Paul so eloquently reminds us, "Do you not know that you are the temple of God, and that the Spirit of God dwells in you?" (1 Cor. 3:16). If our bodies are temples, maintaining them isn't just recommended; it's required.

Imagine your faith journey as a marathon, not a sprint, even though we're steering clear of overused metaphors. The race demands stamina, focus, and refreshment along the way. But how do we ensure our spiritual and emotional well-being in this long run? It's about recognizing that, just as God took a day of rest, we too need to pause and breathe, trusting that the world won't fall apart without our relentless hustle.

The church often encourages us to be self-sacrificing, and rightly so. Sacrifice is central to our understanding of Jesus' love and His ultimate gift. However, it's essential to remember that even Jesus took time to withdraw and pray, as noted in "And when he had sent the multitudes away, he went up on the mountain by himself to pray. Now when evening came, he was alone" (Matt. 14:23). If He, in His divinity and humanity, deemed it necessary to recharge, how much more should we?

One practical approach is to schedule regular "sabbaths" in our week. These are not necessarily full days but pockets of time where we disconnect from the hustle to reconnect with our spiritual selves. This conscious downtime is not idle but a healthy investment in our long-term emotional and spiritual prosperity. These moments of rest can rejuvenate our spirits and refocus our intentions, allowing us to serve more effectively.

Self-care in relation to our faith doesn't mean insulating ourselves from the needs of others. It's more about equipping ourselves to meet those needs with the fullest heart and spirit. We love our neighbors as we love ourselves, and here's the kicker—implied therein is the necessity of self-love and care. Ignoring our own health—mental, emotional, or spiritual—diminishes our ability to truly serve others.

Let's dive a bit deeper into what this can look like. Spiritual disciplines such as prayer, meditation, and scripture reading act as the balance beams for our walk of faith. They're more than just religious practices; they're forms of spiritual self-care. They tune our hearts to God's frequency, reminding us of His peace, which transcends understanding (Phil. 4:7). Through these practices, we're not running on empty but tapping into His inexhaustible well.

Moreover, integrating self-care into our faith life can unleash creativity in how we engage with God. Think about combining prayer with a nature walk, letting the beauty of creation inspire gratitude while getting your body moving. Or mix up scripture study with a bit of journaling, allowing your reflections to spark a dialogue with God.

For some, the concept of self-care may feel selfish or indulgent, especially when juxtaposed with the idea of sacrifice. Yet, consider the oxygen mask philosophy: put on your mask first before assisting others. In the context of faith, ensuring you are spiritually and emotionally nourished allows you to better pour into others' lives, performing acts of service with genuine joy rather than obligation.

So how do we check whether we're truly balancing faith life with self-care? Start by asking yourself: Do I often feel depleted or energized by my commitments? Am I making time to nurture my relationship with God outside structured church activities? Can I find joy and fulfillment in being, as much as in doing?

In essence, finding this balance is about tuning into the rhythm of divine life within us. John 10:10 reminds us that Jesus came that we might have life and have it "more abundantly." Surely, abundant life includes moments of sweet rest and soulful reflection—not just ceaseless action.

Let's embrace the harmony of productivity and peace, ensuring our spiritual flames are fueled, not flickering. It's about aligning our lives so that our walk with God feels more like a graceful dance than a frenzied dash. In doing so, we'll not only conquer the challenges life throws our way but savor the journey as well. Amen to that.

Recognizing and Overcoming Spiritual Burnout

At some point in life, many Christians feel the weight of being overwhelmed, not by worldly concerns, but by the very activities that are meant to uplift: prayer meetings, Bible studies, volunteering, and spreading the gospel. Yes, spiritual burnout is real, and it can sneak up on even the most fervent believer like a Sunday morning alarm clock.

So how do we identify spiritual burnout before it takes hold of our soul like a vine climbing a neglected wall? First, let's recognize that spiritual burnout isn't just about being tired from serving too much. It's about a disconnect, a dimming of the spiritual light that once shone so brightly within. One might find that prayer feels like a chore, Bible reading turns into skimming verses, and enthusiasm for community service dissipates into reluctance.

Recognizing these signs is the first step. Remember, even Elijah, the mighty prophet, experienced a profound sense of fatigue and despair. After his triumphant victory over the prophets of Baal, he sat under a juniper tree, distraught and ready to give up (1 Kings 19:4). It wasn't the outward actions that broke him, but the internal burden he was carrying—showing us that burnout can hit anyone, even those on a mission led by God.

Once we've identified that spiritual burnout is creeping in, we must lean on Biblical principles to overcome it. Jesus himself calls us to come to Him when burdened: "Come to me, all you who labor and are heavy laden, and I will give you rest" (Matt. 11:28). This invitation isn't just about laying our worldly problems at His feet; it also includes our spiritual struggles. It's about seeking refreshment and restoration in Him.

But how do we take proactive steps to rejuvenate our drained spirits? A vital aspect is to reassess and realign our priorities. Instead of focusing on doing things for God, we must first focus on being with God. Just as Martha busied herself and missed the joy of sitting at Jesus' feet like Mary did (Luke 10:38-42), we should prioritize communion with God over endless activity. Let's remind ourselves that our worth doesn't come from what we do for the kingdom but from who we are in Christ.

Embracing rest as a gift rather than a luxury is crucial too. In Genesis, God sets the pace by resting on the seventh day (Gen. 2:2). A Sabbath isn't only about a day off; it's about creating intentional space for spiritual renewal. It's not laziness to rest; it's obedience and wisdom.

Moreover, community plays an imperative role in overcoming burnout. Engaging with a supportive Christian community offers a lifeline when we find ourselves stranded on burnout island. Sharing the burden, just as Aaron and Hur did for Moses by holding up his arms (Exod. 17:12), can restore our strength. Fellowship allows us to carry one another's burdens (Gal. 6:2) and find encouragement in collective worship and shared joy.

Let's dig into one more essential weapon against burnout: rekindling joy and gratitude. The apostle Paul, even amidst hardships, reminded the Thessalonians to "Rejoice evermore. Pray without ceasing. In every thing give thanks" (1 Thess. 5:16-18). When we replace our weariness with gratitude, it shifts our focus from the depletion to the abundance of God's grace.

Conquest

So, if you find yourself slowly treading the waters of spiritual fatigue, remember you're not alone. Even the oak that doesn't break at first feels the strain. Recognize the signs, take them to the Lord, find rest in His presence, lean on your spiritual community, and plant the seeds of joy and gratitude in your heart. Let these truths rejuvenate your spirit and prepare you to stand firm once more, not just as a soldier on duty, but as a conqueror filled with divine zeal.

In moments of weariness, God's invitation to find rest remains as compelling as His command to serve. Spiritual vitality doesn't come from pushing beyond the limits but from savoring the presence of the One who refreshes our souls. Let's press onward, not in our own strength, but guided and renewed by His perfect peace.

Chapter 11:
Embracing Lifelong Growth

As we wade through the river of life, where each ripple whispers the promise of new growth, we realize that growth isn't just a pit stop; it's our lifeline. Spiritual growth, much like good humor, is a delightful necessity — a perpetual metamorphosis fueled by a curiosity to know more about God's love and His plans for us. Our faith, after all, is a vibrant tapestry of continued learning, woven with threads of experience and scripture. The Bible teaches us that "the path of the just is like the shining sun, that shines ever brighter unto the perfect day" (Prov. 4:18). It's an exhilarating revelation that our journey with Christ never plateaus; it's a divine climb towards a horizon that promises eternal wonder. In navigating this luminous path, we toss aside passivity like confetti, engaging actively with our potential and allowing the Holy Spirit to renew our minds daily — a glorious upgrade, if you will, rather like faith getting its version of software updates. So, let's embrace this lifelong growth with a fearless heart and a willing mind, embodying the courage of conquerors, who run their race with tenacity and joy.

Continuous Learning and Development

Life isn't a static journey, and as believers, we're called to embrace growth through continuous learning and development. This isn't an option for Christians—it's a way of life deeply rooted in Scripture. The Bible, with all its wisdom, encourages us to continually seek knowledge and understanding. Proverbs 4:7 declares, "Wisdom is the principal thing; Therefore get wisdom. and in all your getting get understanding" (Prov. 4:7). Now, there's a verse that basically screams "lifelong learning" from the rooftops! Remember wisdom is the correct application of knowledge.

But let's not get ahead of ourselves here. Continuous learning isn't just about cracking open a few books or signing up for a seminary course online—although those are excellent starts. It's about adopting a mindset that's open to change, curious about the divine mysteries, and ready to grow beyond the comfortable confines of our own understanding. It's about stepping out of our comfort zones and allowing the Holy Spirit to lead us down new paths of discovery. As the apostle Paul advises, "Do not be conformed to this world: but be transformed by the renewing of your mind" (Rom. 12:2). Ah, the renewing of the mind—a process as dynamic as it is rewarding.

You might be wondering how continuous learning and development fit into the broader narrative of Christian growth. For starters, it keeps us spiritually fit and ready for the challenges that life throws our way. Just as physical exercise strengthens the body, learning fortifies our spirits. We're not talking just any kind of learning here; we're talking intentional, faith-driven development that aligns with our purpose in Christ. This doesn't just equip us to tackle life; it transforms how we live it. And isn't transformation what being a Christian is all about? If Jesus was big on anything, it was transformation—just ask Lazarus or the woman at the well.

It's easy to get caught up in the idea that learning is a task best left to the young or the scholarly types. But truth be told, God's curriculum is available to all of us, regardless of age or academic qualification. Remember Anna, the prophetess who's been studying God's word and eagerly awaiting the Messiah well into her advanced years? (Luke 2:36-38). Her life isn't just a testament to patience; it's a testament to continuous learning. If Anna could keep her faith muscles toned well into her 80s, surely we can carve out time for spiritual growth, no matter how comfortably we think we've settled into our faith journeys.

So, where do we start this lifelong learning adventure? For one, dive into the Word of God. Let's face it, the Bible is like a bottomless mug of spiritual caffeine—full of new revelations each time you come back to it. Studying scripture isn't just for Sunday school kids or Bible scholars; it's a treasure trove for every believer longing to understand God on a more intimate level. As Paul reminded Timothy, "All scripture is given by inspiration of God, and is profitable for doctrine, for reproof, for correction, for instruction in righteousness" (2 Tim. 3:16). Sounds like a pretty good reason to keep that Bible app pinned on your home screen, doesn't it?

But oh, let's not limit ourselves to just scrolling or flipping pages. Engage with the Word by joining study groups where you can glean insights from others while sharing your own aha moments. Discussing and dissecting scripture with fellow journeyers might open a door to new understandings that solitary study wouldn't have sparked. This collective learning echoes Proverbs 27:17: "Iron sharpens iron; So, a man sharpens the countenance of his friend" (Prov. 27:17).

Outside of study, allow yourself to be mentored and, in turn, become a mentor to others. Mentorship isn't just a business buzzword; it's a Christ-modeled way of life. Jesus Himself spent time teaching and mentoring a ragtag group of disciples who went on to change the world. Imagine if they'd stuck to fishing without the training from our Lord! Engaging in mentoring relationships adds layers to our understanding of God's purpose for us while empowering us to pass on what we've learned—creating a ripple effect of continuous development across generations.

And while we're at it, why not look at the world through a pair of faith-tinted glasses and learn from it too? The core truths of God's creation are all around us, in nature and in the marvels of technology and science. Our God is the author of all wisdom and understanding, and He delights in our pursuit of knowledge. Just remember, while understanding God's creation can enhance our lives, it should always point us back to the Creator Himself. As we grasp worldly knowledge, we should use it to strengthen our heavenly perspectives.

Don't forget to also consider learning from lived experiences—our own and those of others. The Bible is filled with the testimonies of those who've journeyed down challenging paths, and our lives today are filled with stories that carry lessons of perseverance, faith, failure, and redemption. Much like how Elijah learned from solitude at the brook Cherith and Jonah found clarity inside a fish, our own trials can teach us valuable lessons if we remain open to learning from them.

Lastly, never underestimate the power of prayer in the learning process. "If any of you lacks wisdom, let him ask of God, who gives to all liberally, and without reproach and it will be given to him" (James 1:5). Now that's what you call a divine guarantee. We needn't endeavor to learn on our own strength. Seek divine guidance to discern what lessons God wants to impart at any given moment. His wisdom is both illuminating and transformative, helping us to grow in ways that are eternally significant.

Embracing continuous learning and development isn't just a neat personal goal; it's an integral part of living as a conqueror in Christ. As we devote ourselves to lifelong learning, driven by the hope and love of our Savior, we not only prepare ourselves to withstand life's trials, but we're also equipped to contribute to His kingdom. Circle back to Jesus' directive in the parable of the talents. No servant was commended for burying what they were given. They were acknowledged for taking what they had and growing it—and in doing so, they shared in their Master's joy and glory. Let's aim for that eternal acknowledgment, one new lesson at a time.

Staying Relevant in a Changing World

So, you're a modern Christian. You've got your smartphone, maybe a smartwatch, and you've got a never-ending buffet of streaming content. The world is shifting quicker than you can say "WiFi," and it's all too easy to feel left behind if you pause for just a second. But let's not get swept away in the digital tide or simply become reluctant passengers in this speeding train called life. Instead, let's figure out how to stay relevant—and do it with style and a touch of grace that'd make even King Solomon nod in approval.

Now, relevance isn't just about staying updated with the latest tech trends or binge-watching the next big series. It's about making sure that your faith doesn't gather cobwebs in an old attic but shines brightly in your everyday life. Romans 12:2 gives us a timely reminder: "And do not be conformed to this world but be transformed by the renewing of your mind" (Rom. 12:2). Notice that 'renewing your mind' part? That's where the magic happens.

First off, let's talk about the elephant in the room—comfort zones. It's a snuggly place, isn't it? But don't get too cozy. Staying in a comfort zone is like expecting to sail the oceans while anchored to the dock. Sure, you're safe, but you miss the adventure. Remember Caleb in the Old Testament, always ready for the next challenge at an age when most would be thinking about retirement villas (Josh. 14:10-12). Well, the same zest should resonate within us. To stay relevant, taking risks and stepping into uncharted waters is crucial.

Next up: adapt, don't react. The pace of change can sometimes feel like a fire hydrant of information blasting at us. But wait—we've got the 'Fruit of the Spirit' in our arsenal, including patience and self-control (Gal. 5:22-23). Use them to your advantage. When faced with change, reflect on how it aligns with your purpose and calling. Remember, you don't need to know every digital trend, just what serves your mission.

Conquest

Speaking of your mission, staying relevant isn't a solo quest. Get this: we are the sum of our relationships. Who we keep close can either propel us forward or anchor us down. Hebrews 10:24-25 prompts us to "consider one another in order to stir up love and good works" (Heb. 10:24-25). Surround yourself with people who challenge, inspire, and uplift. In doing so, you create a personal think-tank that keeps you sharp and your faith strong.

But of course, not everything should be about wrestling with change. There is also immense value in the timeless. Think of our faith as this unshakeable foundation. The digital age cannot alter the core values of love, kindness, patience, and unyielding faith. When you're anchored on these, you can ride out any storm that comes from a changing world. Remember that the kingdom of Heaven is unshakable.

Maintaining relevance also means being open to learning. The wise men of the Bible weren't wise because they had all the answers—they sought them. Proverbs 1:5 reminds us, "A wise man will hear, and will increase learning; and a man of understanding will attain wise counsels" (Prov. 1:5). Don't shy away from picking up new skills, be it a cooking class, a coding course, or deepening your scriptural knowledge. Growth doesn't happen by accident but through intentional pursuit.

Lastly, let's remember the power of sharing. If keeping your faith vibrant in an evolving world feels daunting, know that storytelling can be a force for both connection and inspiration. Jesus was a master storyteller, using parables that transcend time. A personal anecdote from your life can move others, build bridges, and even spark change. There is an undeniable relevance in authenticity, in showing your journey—warts and all.

So in this whirlwind of a world, let's not get caught in the trap of irrelevance. With faith as our compass and courage our vessel, every storm and sunshine becomes a chapter in God's grand adventure for us. In the words of Paul, "I can do all things through Christ who strengthens me" (Phil. 4:13). Remember, finding relevance isn't about chasing trends but aligning each change with God's purpose for you. Stay curious, stay anchored, and keep sailing strong.

Chapter 12:
Preparing for Eternal Victory

As Christians, our journey doesn't culminate with an earthly resolution; rather, it crescendos with the promise of eternal victory, a divine inheritance that withstands the test of time. This chapter propels us into the essence of embracing our God-given destiny, fueled by a faith that conquers all. By wrapping our hearts around the hope of forever, we equip ourselves with a warrior's mindset, breaking free from the notion of passive existence and marching boldly towards the ultimate conquest. The scriptures remind us, "But thanks be to God, who gives us the victory through our Lord Jesus Christ" (1 Cor. 15:57). Keeping this promise deeply ingrained in our souls becomes our greatest weapon against complacency and despondence. Living with an eternal perspective shifts our gaze from temporary trials to everlasting triumphs, transforming every act of kindness and faith into steps on the path to everlasting joy. Our lives become a canvas where His love paints the colors of victory, illuminating even the darkest corridors of our earthly pilgrimage. So, let's don our spiritual armor, rally one another with encouraging tales of faith, and stride forward with hearts ever expectant of the glorious eternity before us.

Understanding the Promise of Eternal Life

As we journey through this life like explorers charting unknown territories, we often ponder one of life's greatest mysteries—what happens after we exhale for the last time? For believers, the concept of eternal life isn't just a celestial consolation prize handed out in the sweeping realms of the afterlife. No, it's a promise as concrete and palpable as the ground beneath our feet. Eternal life is a cornerstone of Christian faith, not merely a footnote.

In some ways, the idea of eternal life can feel like looking at the stars on a clear night—infinitely distant yet intimately personal. The staggering promise Jesus offers in the Book of John is hard to ignore: "Most assuredly, I say to you, He who believes in me has everlasting life" (John 6:47). This isn't a fleeting promise or a checked box on a cosmic to-do list. It's an invitation to a continual relationship with the Creator, both here and beyond the veil of death.

When we talk about living in victory, we're talking about more than surviving another day—it's about embodying this promise of eternity, right here, right now. After all, God didn't send His Son to offer us mere survival; He aimed for abundance! Jesus said, "I am come that they might have life, and that they might have it more abundantly" (John 10:10). Take a moment to consider that abundance in the context of eternity—not confined to lifespans, conditions, or circumstances.

But how do we reconcile this promise with the sometimes dreary trek of everyday existence? Our lives can often seem like a series of mundane and trivial events, each one drawing us further from those extraordinary moments we expect as believers. Here's where the divine sense of humor kicks in. Imagine God's whisper—"Yes, your everyday life is part of the journey!" It's about finding sprint-like moments of grace and joy woven into the marathon of life. No need to complicate it. Simplicity often reveals profound truths.

Embrace the paradox—eternal life starts now, yet it never ends. Such a truth can feel both freeing and daunting. Many of us think of eternity like a never-ending worship service, a serene scene straight out of a stained glass window. But it's more dynamic and vibrant than our wildest imaginations can conceive. Picture life everlasting, not lived out in a gray celestial waiting room, but growing, dancing, and evolving with divine purpose and intent.

Incorporating eternal life into your daily walk flips your so-called mundane tasks into acts of worship and faith. Cook a meal? Offer thanks for the provisions. Help a neighbor? Delight in the shared human experience. Each action, no matter how seemingly insignificant, contributes to the grander tapestry of eternity. Paul tells us in his letter to the Corinthians, "For we walk by faith, not by sight" (2 Cor. 5:7). This faith walk starts in the here and now, paving the way toward and through eternity.

The good news is, understanding eternal life doesn't require a theology degree or even a hard-to-decipher secret map. It's present in our core doctrine and exemplified by Jesus Himself. His resurrection was the ultimate plot twist, the event that rewrote the end game: "But now Christ is risen from the dead and has become the firstfruits of those who have fallen asleep" (1 Cor. 15:20). It's the quintessential victory through which we glimpse the potential of eternal life.

Rather than a faraway dream, eternal life beckons us to live with purpose, transforming not just how we view the future but how we inhabit the present. There's a great comfort in knowing that our lives tether us to God's everlasting plan. It's this very promise that emboldens us to engage in trials and tribulations with renewed vigor and strength. Our battles aren't futile when waged with the backdrop of eternity.

Friends, eternity doesn't just extend life; it enriches it. We get the remarkable opportunity to deepen our knowledge, grow our faith, and expand love's depths forever. Imagine waking up each day with a sense of peace and direction because you know your life threads into an eternal tapestry far more colorful than any earthly masterpiece. You hold the needle and thread in your actions and choices.

The promise of eternal life also calls us to rise above a passive existence, to cherish every fleeting moment while holding onto the everlasting essence of our Creator. Paul's letter to the Romans offers this wisdom: "But if the Spirit of him who raised Jesus from the dead dwells in you, he who raised Christ from the dead will also give life to your mortal bodies through his Spirit who dwells in you" (Rom. 8:11). The Spirit residing within is both a promise and a present—a precursor to life everlasting.

Let this eternal victory ripple through every aspect of your earthly walk. Engage with people as if each interaction stretches into forever. Hug tightly, listen deeply, and love fiercely. In this way, we understand the promise of eternal life not as a distant ideal but as an affirmed reality to manifest today.

Living with an Eternal Perspective

We spend so much time looking at our watches, waiting for that meeting to end or that lunch break to finally arrive. Our lives seem bound by the ticking of the clock, don't they? Yet, as Christians, we're invited to lift our eyes to a timeline that stretches into eternity. Living with an eternal perspective isn't just a spiritual concept—it's a profound shift in how we navigate the ups and downs of life.

Consider this: The circumstances we face, whether mundane or monumental, are fleeting when compared to eternity. The Apostle Paul encourages us, "While we do not look at the things which are seen, but at the things which are not seen. For the things which are seen are temporary; but the things which are not seen are eternal" (2 Cor. 4:18). This perspective is not about disengaging from our earthly concerns but rather infusing those concerns with everlasting significance.

With all life's distractions, it's easy to fall into the trap of living as if today is all there is. We've got bills to pay, kids to drive to soccer practice, and let's not forget that report due first thing Monday morning. Yet, the call to view life through an eternal lens invites us to see beyond our current pressures and gain a sense of purpose that transcends daily obligations.

When we adopt an eternal perspective, we're not ignoring the reality around us. Instead, we're choosing to frame it within God's ultimate purpose. This isn't a ticket to a carefree life, but it is a guide to peace amidst the chaos. The Bible is filled with accounts of those who kept their eyes fixed on what lies beyond, like Abraham who sought "a city which has foundations, whose builder and maker is God" (Heb. 11:10).

Now, let's sprinkle in a little humor here—think of life as a grand buffet, even the desserts. We might be tempted to fill our plates with the most delicious items right in front of us, but someone who understands an eternal perspective knows to leave room for the real feast to come—an everlasting one.

This eternal perspective isn't built in isolation. It is enriched through community and fellowship, as discussed in earlier chapters. Sharing our hopes, dreams, and fears within our Christian circles strengthens our understanding and commitment to this perspective. When we confront loss or disappointment, having others remind us of the heavenly promises can be a balm to our souls.

So, how exactly do we cultivate this perspective? One way is by feeding our minds with Scripture. The Bible continually grounds us in the realities of eternity. "Set your mind on things above, not on things on the earth" (Col. 3:2), urges Paul, reminding us that our hearts should seek what lasts forever. Reading, meditating, and reflecting on God's word anchors our soul in His promises.

Prayer, our personal communication line with God, also sharpens our focus on eternal matters. Through prayer, we align our will with

His, transforming our desires from temporal to everlasting. This practice, detailed in the chapter on building a strong prayer life, is indispensable in maintaining an eternal perspective.

Living with an eternal perspective inherently alters our values and priorities. We begin to invest in love, generosity, and kindness—values that resonate into eternity. When Jesus taught to store up treasures in heaven, He wasn't merely giving financial advice. He was challenging us to build a portfolio that carries eternal dividends (Matt. 6:19-21).

Furthermore, living with eternity in mind propels us to action. We become stewards of God's kingdom here on earth. It's as if each day is an opportunity to create ripples that extend into eternity. Whether it's through sharing the gospel, acts of service, or simply living out our faith authentically, our actions start echoing into the beyond.

Let's also talk about the trials and tribulations. They're part and parcel of the earthly journey. However, when viewed through the eternal lens, these challenges become opportunities for growth and faith. "For our light affliction, which is but for a moment, is working for us a far more exceeding and eternal weight of glory" (2 Cor. 4:17). Suddenly, the struggle isn't just a struggle; it's a chance to develop perseverance and deepen our reliance on God.

In essence, an eternal perspective recalibrates our life's compass. It's the difference between seeing storms as overwhelming hurdles or as passing waves that are shaping us for the future God has designed.

But let's keep it real. Maintaining an eternal focus isn't always easy. It requires discipline, a continual renewing of our minds, and sometimes, a good dose of humor to keep us grounded. Yet, when we slip, God's grace always brings us back, prompting us to re-evaluate and recommit.

So, take a pause. Reflect on what in your life has eternal value. It's not about being perfect; it's about being persistent in pursuing what

Conquest

truly matters. "For where your treasure is, there your heart will be also" (Matt. 6:21). Choose wisely, invest in what lasts, and find hope that's unwavering—it's not just for the here and now, but for forever.

Conclusion

As we reach the end of this journey, there sits an undeniable truth; your path as a Christian conqueror is not just a title but a lifelong invitation. Unlike a book's pages that eventually reach their final turn, your walk with Christ is an ongoing narrative, penned with the ink of faith, bold actions, and a community empowered through prayer and purpose. Having explored how our identity in Christ shapes us, it's time to reflect on how this knowledge transforms into action. The Christian life isn't meant to be passive or resigned; it's a call to rise as active participants in God's grand tapestry, crafted with purpose and promise.

The Apostle Paul once wrote, "I can do all things through Christ who strengthens me" (Phil. 4:13). This isn't a mere motivational mantra—it's foundational truth. God's power working in us allows us to face challenges head-on, eschewing passive complacency. We are not victims of circumstance but victors by divine design. It's this realization that compels us to transition from mere spectators to proactive partners in the Kingdom's advancement.

Perhaps the most stirring realization from our exploration is the dynamic power of the Holy Spirit. The Spirit isn't an ethereal afterthought but a comforting guide and mighty enabler. With gifts and fruits vividly flourishing in our lives, we're better equipped to serve, discern, and love more deeply. The early church turned the world upside down with this empowerment; why shouldn't we? It is our privilege and responsibility to actively listen and follow the Spirit's lead.

Conquest

Prayer, undoubtedly, emerges as the anchor amidst storms. In our journey, we've underscored its transformative power. Whether in whispered moments of solitude or fervent communal gatherings, prayer is our lifeline, the divine conversation that fuels our faith and fortifies our resolve. Effective prayer isn't about the eloquence of our words but the sincerity of our hearts. As we cultivate this communion, we're reminded of James's assertion, "The effective, fervent prayer of a righteous man avails much" (James 5:16).

Community forms the bedrock of our faith walk. We've learned that Christianity is not a solo endeavor but a collective melody played by hearts in harmonious unity. Together, we are stronger, mirroring the early church's devotion to fellowship and mutual care. In building supportive Christian relationships, not only do we find strength, but we also offer it, fostering an environment of growth and accountability.

Reflecting on life's unavoidable challenges, we are encouraged to view trials not as insurmountable mountains but as opportunities for divine demonstration. It's in our adversity that resilience is born, faith is tested, and testimonies are crafted. Shadrach, Meshach, and Abednego walked through the fire not alone but alongside their God, emerging unharmed—a powerful reminder that we, too, are never alone in our trials.

The power of personal testimony cannot be overstated. Each story of faith, each encounter with grace serves as a beacon for others, lighting the path to hope and encouragement. By sharing our journeys, we become relatable witnesses to the transformative power of the Gospel, inviting others into the warmth of God's overwhelming love.

Living faith in action ties the essence of our belief to tangible deeds, echoing James's sentiment that "faith without works is dead" (James 2:26). Our actions must be the living manifestation of the faith we profess. We are called to impact society profoundly, seeking justice, loving mercy, and walking humbly with our God. The mark of a true believer isn't in grand declarations but quiet consistency.

In managing our spiritual and emotional health, balance emerges as a key theme. While passionate zeal should fuel our endeavors, it's essential to nurture our inner well-being. Recognizing burnout not as a sign of weakness but as a reminder to retreat and recharge, we embrace the Sabbath's principle—offering rest to our weary souls, drawing from the wellspring of Christ's peace.

Embracing lifelong growth keeps us agile in an ever-evolving world. Continuous learning ensures we remain relevant, adaptable, and equipped to engage with an increasingly complex society. Cultivating a curious heart and an open mind allows us to seek new understandings and embrace fresh perspectives, all while grounded in the unchanging truths of Scripture.

Finally, preparing for eternal victory reminds us of the greatest promise yet to come. Living with an eternal perspective infuses our transient moments with purpose. It shifts the focus from earthly possessions to heavenly treasures, from temporal struggles to eternal triumphs. Christ's victory is ours to share, a crown of promise waiting just beyond the horizon.

As stewards of this message, let's go forth with humor that disarms, motivation that compels, and inspiration that lifts. Our tale isn't one of defeat but of divine conquest, crafted by the Almighty Author whose final chapter hasn't yet been written. Embrace this adventure, clothe yourselves with courage, and set your gaze upward, for the best is yet to come. We are conquerors, and this is just the beginning. Amen.

Made in the USA
Middletown, DE
04 April 2025

73641234R00055